*Theatre in the Age of Irving*

D1589511

*Drama and Theatre Studies*

GENERAL EDITOR: KENNETH RICHARDS
ADVISORY EDITOR: HUGH HUNT

Theatre in Ireland
MICHEÁL Ó hAODHA

A Short History of Scene Design in Britain
SYBIL ROSENFELD

Theatre in the Age of Kean
JOSEPH DONOHUE

GEORGE ROWELL

# *Theatre in the Age of Irving*

Basil Blackwell · Oxford

First published 1981
Basil Blackwell Publisher Ltd
108 Cowley Road
Oxford OX4 1JF
England

*British Library Cataloguing in Publication Data*

Rowell, George
    Theatre in the age of Irving. — (Drama and
    theatre studies)
    1.  Theatre — England — History — 19th century
    I.  Title      II.  Series
    792'.0942      PN2594

    ISBN 0-631-10711-8

Typesetting in 12 on 13½ pt Atlantic by Pioneer Associates, Flimwell
Printed and Bound in Great Britain by Billing and Sons Ltd, Guildford
and Kemp Hall Bindery, Oxford

# Contents

# Illustrations

# *Preface*

The late Victorian period has shown itself to hold a particular appeal for those who live a hundred years later. In one sense it is 'modern'; its people travelled extensively by train, its men wore daily the clothes still occasionally donned — for weddings or funerals; the privileged used telephones and switched on electric light. But these outward signs of twentieth-century living covered a social, economic, and artistic world entirely different from our own. To study the age has therefore the attraction of thumbing through the family album: the scenes and faces are both recognisable and remote, a fascinating combination.

The same sense of watching a world still just surviving clings to the study of its theatre. Some of the homes the Victorian actors and managers created for themselves prosper today: Wyndham's, Her Majesty's (built by Tree), the Palace (opened as the English Opera House by D'Oyly Carte) — but others have been demolished (the St James's, raised to its zenith by Alexander) or debased (the Lyceum, Irving's own home), and the actor-manager himself has gone. In the provinces a handful of 'No. 1 dates' still operate, but scores of Victorian theatres which once housed touring companies have vanished. There is a bitter-sweet satisfaction in studying a theatrical way of life that seems unlikely to continue into the twenty-first century.

I am therefore particularly grateful to Basil Blackwell for their invitation to contribute this book to their 'Drama and Theatre Studies'; to Kenneth Richards for his encouragement at every stage of its writing; and to him and Hugh Hunt for their helpful comments on the typescript. I owe a special debt to Michael Booth, who allowed me to read his chapter on 'Irving's *Faust*' before its publication in his study, *Victorian Spectacular Theatre*.

I count myself fortunate to have been able to work throughout the book's preparation in the Library of the Garrick Club, a building graced by so many leading figures in the theatre of the period, and to have been allowed to use its resources for the illustrations. My thanks are also due to Norman Philbrick for kindly agreeing to the inclusion of pictorial material from the Philbrick Library.

Any student of Henry Irving finds his sheet-anchor in the biography by his grandson, *Henry Irving: The Actor and His World*. Laurence Irving's book and Ellen Terry's *Memoirs*, surely the least vain and most valuable of actor's autobiographies, are the records of a theatrical era on which I have drawn deepest and from which I have learnt most. I am glad to acknowledge my debt.

# CHAPTER ONE

# Setting the Scene

'Winning fame in a night' is a theatrical feat more often written about than achieved. A little-known performer may carry a first-night audience before him and reap a harvest of critical praise next day, but unless he sustains that first success, history will very soon lose sight of him. Even rarer is the actor who in a single night makes himself not merely famous but foremost in his profession. In the annals of the English theatre three names stand unchallenged for such an achievement: David Garrick as Richard III; Edmund Kean as Shylock; and Henry Irving as Mathias in *The Bells*.

From the date (25 November 1871) of Irving's first appearance in that part to the date (13 October 1905) of his last appearance on the stage, which was also the date of his death, his hold on the theatrical public was universally recognised — as much by his detractors, who were many, as by his admirers, who were more. Both his own and succeeding generations have agreed that the last thirty years of the nineteenth century were the age of Irving, a distinction recognised in 1895 when he became the first actor-knight. At the same time his achievement was by no means limited to self-advancement. He saw his task as far wider than making the Lyceum a National Theatre in all but name; his ambition was to make the English theatre as a whole a national institution, universally recognised and universally respected. The measure of his success in this aim lies not only in his own knighthood but also in the honours subsequently conferred on his competitors: on Bancroft, Wyndham, Hare, Tree, Alexander, and in the fullness of time on his partner, Ellen Terry. The record of the theatre in Irving's day is primarily the history of the Lyceum, but it is also the history of these actors, and of the hundreds in the profession who drew inspiration from his example and support from his success.

It was fashionable in Irving's lifetime to draw attention to the actor's peculiar physique and manner. His long, lean figure provided the cartoonist with an irresistible target, and his acting style invited imitation wherever two or three playgoers were gathered together, from artistic families like the Du Mauriers, with young Gerald 'imitating Irving up and down the passages of Harrow',[1] to the humble home of the Grossmiths' Mr Pooter, exposed to 'the Irving business' for three nights in succession by the stage-struck Mr Burwin-Fosselton. What invites comment a century later, however, is not so much the actor snatching success from the jaws of ridicule as the manager guiding the fortunes of the Lyceum against the prevailing currents of European drama. Irving's triumphs were won in a mixture of Shakespeare and melodrama — often Shakespeare *as* melodrama — whereas the mainstream of new drama during these years flowed strongly in the direction of naturalism, with Zola, Strindberg, and above all Ibsen as the representative playwrights of the epoch. Even in England the decade preceding Irving's emergence was notable chiefly for the 'cup and saucer' comedies of Robertson as staged by the Bancrofts at the Prince of Wales's — naturalism on a miniature scale compared with Ibsen or Strindberg but equally remote from the Lyceum repertoire.

Irving's chosen course may therefore be said to run counter to the new dramatic movements in both Europe and England. Put more positively, he established and sustained in England a Romantic drama comparable to that of Goethe and Schiller in Germany and Hugo and Dumas in France half a century earlier. The greatest paradox of his career is not so much his achievement of this Romantic renaissance without the physical advantages upon which Romantic actors rely, but its achievements without Romantic dramatists. Certainly he had reason to be grateful to Shakespeare (though his critics doubted whether Shakespeare had reason to be grateful to him), but he never found — and perhaps never sought — his own Shakespeare. His *Faust* was not Goethe's, nor his *Don Quixote* Cervantes', but the work of the same man: the once ubiquitous, now forgotten, W.G. Wills. For the most part when choosing writers, Irving looked backward rather than round about. Even Tennyson was something of a voice from the past by the time he was heard on the Lyceum stage, and *Becket* waited fifteen years for its posthumous production.

Given Irving's unique qualities as an actor — a blend of sardonic humour and hypnotic power, veiled always in mystery — it has been assumed that this course of events was inevitable; that he was not the actor, nor the Lyceum the theatre, to achieve greatness in drawing-room drama, stiff-collared and frock-coated. But was his choice of costume parts in period plays so firmly predestined? The crossroads of Irving's career may be identified not as the first night of *The Bells*, but as his decision six months earlier to leave the company at the Vaudeville Theatre. There he had scored the success of the season in *Two Roses* by James Albery — perhaps the most Robertsonian comedy not to be written by Robertson. Irving played Digby Grant, the engaging if devious father of the two roses of the title, and as fully frock-coated a character as the English repertoire then afforded.

Once the London run was over, the company embarked on an extended tour which took them in May 1871 to the Theatre Royal, Dublin. Here during a crowded two-week run they were seen by a red-headed schoolboy, still two months short of his fifteenth birthday, yet already a confirmed playgoer with strong likes and dislikes where the theatre was concerned. The boy's current favourite was Barry Sullivan, an itinerant tragedian whom he was later to describe as 'the last of the heroic figures who had dominated the stage since the palmy Siddons-Kemble days'.[2] Nothing could contrast more strongly with the Titanic figure of Sullivan in Shakespeare than Irving as Digby Grant, who struck his young critic as 'an actor with a tall thin figure which if it could not be convicted of grotesqueness was certainly indescribably peculiar, and a voice which was dependent so much on the resonance of a cavernous nose that it was, compared to the powerful chest voice of Barry Sullivan, a highly cultivated neigh'.[3]

Yet the schoolboy, who was to eclipse the fame of either Sullivan or Irving and who answered to the name of Shaw, recognised,

3

despite the thin figure and thinner voice, the actor who would dominate the London stage for the next thirty years. Moreover, though he remained convinced that Sullivan was the supreme exponent of Shakespeare, the seed was sown that night of a belief that Irving would prove the perfect interpreter of the drama of tomorrow.

> I instinctively felt that a new drama inhered in this man, though I had no conscious notion that I was destined to write it; and I perceive now that I never forgave him for baffling the plans I made for him (always, be it remembered, unconsciously) . . .
> Here, I felt, is something that leaves the old stage and its super-stitions and staleness completely behind, and inaugurates a new epoch in the theatre.[4]

But the crossroads had already been reached and the crucial turning taken. Before starting on the *Two Roses* tour Irving had signed with Bateman to play leading roles at the Lyceum, and it was at the Lyceum in Shakespeare and melodrama that Shaw found him when he arrived in London five years later. His disillusion was bitter — far from sponsoring the birth of a new drama, Irving had 'immediately turned back to the old Barry Sullivan repertory of mutilated Shakespeare and Bulwer Lytton',[5] and his offence was shortly compounded by engaging as his coadjutor the actress Shaw most admired, Ellen Terry.

Nor can he have found much comfort elsewhere in the London theatre. That new drama of which he had instinctively recognised the progenitor in Irving was lamentably slow in arriving. *Two Roses* proved to be among the last blossoms in the Robertsonian summer, for Robertson himself died in 1871, while the play was running, and Albery, his presumed heir, drifted uncertainly to an early grave. English drama in the 1870s and 1880s was characterised by a widespread dependence on the contemporary French stage, and even the Bancrofts found their new successes in Paris, with repeated adaptations of Sardou for such favourites as *Diplomacy, Odette* and *Fédora.* It was this second-hand and second-rate element in English dramatic fare that Shaw stigmatised as 'Sardoodledom' when he succeeded to the post of dramatic critic of the *Saturday Review* in 1895.

Both Shaw and those historians who follow him have, however, overlooked the maxim that theatrical reform must precede dramatic development. Before a dramatist as original as Ibsen or Shaw himself could be heard, the theatre had to be transformed: new buildings, new actors, above all new audiences were needed. The 1870s and 1880s are usually regarded as a period of anticlimax in the history of the English stage, but if the Bancrofts' work is judged as theatrical reform, and not limited to their encouragement of Robertsonian comedy, a kinder view can be taken. Their achievements at the Prince of Wales's were sustained elsewhere: their own move to the Haymarket in 1880 brought new standards to the heart of theatrical London, and their colleagues, Hare and the Kendals, carried through a similar flanking movement, occupying first an outpost, the Court Theatre in Sloane Square, and then moving invincibly on Mayfair and the St James's. Meanwhile their contemporary, Charles Wyndham, had established himself at the Criterion, underneath Piccadilly Circus, 'the heart of the Empire', from which he was later to extend his own empire by building Wyndham's and the New theatres.

The history of the English stage in these years is therefore one of theatrical progress, if dramatic inertia. The advances were chiefly in the art of presentation; the gilding of the Haymarket proscenium as a 'picture-frame' is sometimes mocked as constituting the Bancrofts' crowning glory, but it represented the aim of all the leading impresarios of the age — to bring theatrical art, for long scorned or at best tolerated by patrons of the other arts, to an acceptable and competitive level of achievement. Irving's magic and mystery at the Lyceum, Hare's and the Kendals' drawing-room dramas at the St James's, Wyndham's 'sophisticated' farces at the Criterion (with the bedroom discreetly in the wings) were all part of this process.

One theatrical enterprise of the period needs more specific consideration. Both satire and the musical stage had proved doggedly derivative in the preceding century and a half. Censorship, statutorily established by the Licensing Act of 1737, drove stage satire inward on itself, so that the theatre could only pillory the theatre. Successions of foreign composers invaded the orchestra-pit: Handel, Mozart, Weber, provided German music, Bellini, Donizetti, Verdi, Italian. The English could only offer in competition ballad-opera, burlesque, and extravaganza. But those audiences whom the actor-managers attracted in the 1860s and 1870s looked for something less parochial and salacious than burlesque, and less exotic than foreign opera. It was this taste that the Gilbert and Sullivan operas increasingly fed, originally at the Opera Comique, then at the Savoy, which they created with D'Oyly Carte. The Savoy Operas reflect perfectly the theatrical tone of the 1880s: intelligent but not intellectual, discerning but not demanding, tuneful but not cloying — a 'divine emollient' for the well-educated and well-to-do.

Once the theatre had advanced and the audience was encouraged, the climate was established for dramatic development. In true British fashion this stemmed from the most popular forms of drama, melodrama and farce, the staple fare of the nineteenth-century bill. Pinero contributed a series of farces at once homely and humorous, then turned his attention to the more solemn 'problem play'; Henry Arthur Jones, a successful practitioner of melodrama in the 1880s, moved into smarter sets and a more rigid code with his fashionable comedies of the 1890s; Oscar Wilde, waking to the potential of the theatre as a rich repository for his paradoxes and a richer vein for his creditors, produced the four hardiest plays amongst the Society drama of this period.

It was this fully-fledged theatre of the actor-managers' era that Shaw attacked from his siege-platform on the *Saturday Review*. Perhaps not even Shaw expected the response to be a Lyceum *Masterbuilder* or *John Gabriel Borkman,* but in 1896 he contrived another crossroads for Irving by offering him in *The Man of Destiny* a chance to play Napoleon in the kind of costume-piece the Lyceum audience relished, with a part for Ellen Terry which matched (in the author's view) the talents of that lady. If Irving had acquiesced for his partner's sake . . . ? It is tantalising to rearrange theatrical history: Irving as Captain Brassbound, converted by Terry as Lady Cicely? Irving as Caesar or General Burgoyne? Tantalising, but vain, since Irving rejected Shaw's Napoleon in favour of Sardou's, with Terry as Madame Sans-Gêne. 'Sardoodledom' was not ready to yield at the first whiff of grapeshot.

Nevertheless the limitations of the Lyceum repertoire combined with the conservative taste of other actor-managers to strengthen the resistance movement which called for an intellectual drama worthy of an intelligent audience. Confined at first to the occasional offering of the Independent Theatre and its successor, the Stage Society, this new audience had grown sufficiently by the early 1900s to support a full-scale season at the Court. In the summer of 1905 Irving played at Drury Lane in what proved to be his last London appearances. The programme, *Becket, The Merchant of Venice, A Story of Waterloo,* and *Louis XI,* had a distinct flavour of 'mutilated Shakespeare and Bulwer Lytton', as the young Shaw had termed it. At the same time the stage of the Court was occupied by *Candida, You Never Can Tell, John Bull's Other Island,* and *Man and Superman.* Shaw as a dramatist had arrived, but the 'new drama' of which he had once believed Irving capable had passed into the hands of the young actor playing Marchbanks, Valentine, Keegan, and John Tanner: Harley Granville-Barker.

Four months later on the stage of the Theatre Royal, Bradford, Irving spoke the last lines of *Becket*: 'Into Thy Hands, O Lord, into Thy Hands'. Within an hour he had died. In London at the Court that day they had played a matinee of *The Return of the Prodigal,* given *John Bull's Other Island* in the evening, and rehearsed *The Wild Duck.* Irving's day — the age of the actor — was over. The age of the dramatist had begun.

NOTES

1  Daphne du Maurier, *Gerald: A Portrait* (1934), p. 51.
2  Christopher St John (Editor), *Ellen Terry and Bernard Shaw: A Correspondence* (1949), p. xxi.
3  Ibid., p. xxiv.
4  Ibid., p. xxv.
5  Ibid., p. xxvi.

# CHAPTER TWO

# Lord of the Lyceum

In quitting the smart new Vaudeville, firmly established on the success of *Two Roses*, to join Bateman at the Lyceum, Henry Irving, already thirty-three, was risking his recently acquired reputation. The theatre itself, despite its long history and impressive portico, had never enjoyed steady prosperity and had bankrupted several of its earlier managers, including the once triumphant Madame Vestris and her husband, Charles James Mathews. It had in fact been dark for six months prior to Bateman's tenancy. Irving's new manager, impressively baptised Hezekiah Linthicum, had devoted himself to furthering the theatrical careers of his family, and in particular two of his daughters, Kate and Isabel, upon whom his plans for the Lyceum chiefly rested. Neither was happily cast as a leading lady. Kate, an actress of undoubted if unrefined power, and acceptable as Lady Macbeth or Queen Margaret, was not designed for audiences to cherish. Isabel, not yet seventeen, was a diffident performer who presently complicated matters by falling in love with her leading man. It was evidently to compensate for her inexperience that Bateman engaged the most successful comic actor of the previous season.

Certainly the immediate use he made of his new recruit suggested a misjudgment of that actor's powers. Digby Grant in *Two Roses* was a snobbish and scheming adventurer who exploited family and friends to implement his pretensions, and Irving had given a richly detailed account of his devious conduct. In *Fanchette, or Will o' the Wisp* (written by Mrs Bateman to display the modest talents of her daughter, Isabel), he found himself cast as a Breton peasant besotted by a heroine half his age. When this unlikely drama failed to draw the public, Bateman fell back on Dickens, the standby of so many Victorian managers, and offered a hotch-potch dramatisation of *Pickwick Papers* in which Irving's gift for grotesque comedy found some outlet in the antics of Alfred Jingle, without saving the piece or the enterprise. Had any theatrical prophet forecast at this point that the impersonator of Landry Barbeau and Jingle would shortly make himself leader of the acting profession in a repertoire nicely balanced between Shakespeare and historical romance, he would have astonished the lessee of the Lyceum no less than the playgoing public.

Bateman's reluctance to honour his promise and bring forward Irving in an adaptation of *Le Juif Polonais* was therefore understandable. It is true that before *Two Roses* the actor had chiefly impressed London audiences by his playing of melodramatic villains such as Rawdon Scudamore in Boucicault's *Hunted Down* and (most recently) Compton Kerr in *Formosa*, also by Boucicault, at Drury Lane. But these were modern melodramas, dressed in smart contemporary suits and settings. *Le Juif Polonais* derived from the *Contes et Romans Alsaciens* of Erckmann and Chatrian, and Leopold Lewis's adaptation laid some stress on place and period. Mathias, the central character, was a middle-aged burgomaster and innkeeper, quite outside Irving's previous range of melodramatic villains. Even riskier was the play's emphasis on the tension developing in Mathias's mind. All the drama, even the obligatory sensation scenes (the 'vision' of the murdered Jew and the trial scene), were products of a tormented imagination. Indeed the rival version of the play (*Paul Zegers* by F.C. Burnand) which opened — and failed — at the Alfred Theatre while *The Bells* was in rehearsal presented the events of the drama as a dream from which the condemned man was happily awakened by his wife. Leopold Lewis's adaptation with its tragic ending placed an enormous burden on the interpreter of Mathias, since the conflicts involved were consistently internal. To the other participants, the story of *The Bells* is simply that of a wedding

9

celebration unhappily spoilt by the illness and death of the bride's father. They remain wholly oblivious of the significance in this distressing event of the long-lost Polish Jew.

Irving's triumph on the first night, the suspense he transmitted in the mesmerist scene and the appalling reality of his death throes, have become part of theatre history, rendered all the more haunting by the knowledge that this triumph coincided with the irrevocable breakdown of his marriage. As they drove home past Hyde Park Corner, the wife who had never fully accepted her translation from Surgeon-General's daughter to actor's wife and now saw that fate sealed by the evening's outcome, exclaimed: 'Are you going on making a fool of yourself like this all your life?' Her husband stopped the carriage, got out and turned his back on her for good, encompassing professional acclaim and personal disaster in one evening. Undoubtedly the personal disaster served to fuel his professional progress. All the dreams of happiness shared and domesticity enjoyed which marriage had seemed to offer were sacrificed on the altar of ambition. That extraordinary daemon which friends and foes alike recognised in Irving's work at the Lyceum sprang from the midnight moment of truth at Hyde Park Corner. The success of *The Bells* had secured his reputation as an actor; the contempt with which Florence Irving dismissed his achievement set him on the path to leadership of the English theatre, international fame, and the first theatrical knighthood.

In another respect his triumph in *The Bells* laid the foundations of his subsequent career by identifying him with melodrama strongly coloured by mystery and the supernatural. As has been seen, his immediate successes before moving to the Lyceum were either in comic roles displaying social pretensions (Reginald Chevenix in *Uncle Dick's Darling*, Digby Grant) or in contemporary villainy. Certainly Bateman had glimpsed what his protegé could do in a darkly mysterious vein when he heard Irving recite Hood's poem, 'The Dream of Eugene Aram'. But Mathias was his first full-length essay in the portrayal of the strangely sinister, a note he was to touch again and again in the roles that succeeded Mathias: Eugene Aram in Wills's dramatisation of the story; Richelieu; Louis XI; Dubosc in *The Lyons Mail*; Mephistopheles, as well as several of his Shakespearean parts.

Such roles brought out his strength and concealed his weakness.

Irving's limitations have been endlessly criticised: the spindly legs and crablike walk; the curious West Country vowels and inflexibly nasal tone of voice 'which was' in the words of Shaw already quoted 'dependent so much on the resonance of a cavernous nose that is was, compared to the powerful and musical chest voice of Barry Sullivan, a highly cultivated neigh'.[1] To these defects were often added his lack of power and pace in emotional scenes, and the frequent interjections, threatening rhythm and even sense, as an American journalist showed by transcribing (vividly if unkindly) Irving's treatment of two lines from *The Merchant of Venice*:

> Wa thane, ett no eperes
> Ah! um! yo ned m'elp.
> Ough! ough! Gaw too thane! Ha! um!
> Yo com'n say
> Ah! Shilock! Um! ouch! we wode hev moanies![2]

Irving himself not only knew his limitations but how to use them. Mathias's last line in the published text of *The Bells* reads: 'The rope! The rope! Cut the rope!' Gordon Craig, however, records how Irving changed them to 'Take the rope from my neck' or rather 'Tack the rup frum mey neck' to suggest the last gasps of the hangman's victim.[3] Thus melodrama in a mysterious and menacing vein remained in his repertoire year after year: not only *The Bells* but *The Lyons Mail* (with its strongly contrasted dual role), *The Corsican Brothers* (another dual role and a 'ghost melody' for good measure), *Eugene Aram, Louis XI, Faust,* and others. Ellen Terry remembered that once on a long American train journey she was intrigued by Irving's enigmatic expression and asked him what he was thinking about.

> 'I was thinking,' he answered slowly, 'how strange it is that I should have made the reputation I have as an actor, with nothing to help me — with no equipment. My legs, my voice — everything has been against me. For an actor who can't walk, can't talk, and has no face to speak of, I've done pretty well.'[4]

Of course he possessed unique gifts as well as singular shortcomings: above all, commanding eyes set in an eloquent face. He was by no means confined to the strange and sinister. He could convey majesty, nobility, saintliness, though he found simplicity difficult, and after battling successfully to present the childlike trust of the Vicar of Wakefield, was heard to bleat 'Baa! baa!' in the wings.[5] But goodness elevated to martyrdom involved no such problems: as Charles I going to his execution or Lesurques in *The Lyons Mail* braving the guillotine he could move multitudes. After recording his answer to her question, Ellen Terry adds:

> And I looking, at that splendid head, those wonderful hands, the whole strange beauty of him, thought, 'Ah, you little know.'[6]

Irving's emergence as the foremost actor of the time restored the fortunes of the Lyceum. When Bateman's widow surrendered the lease in 1878, she generously referred in her press statement to 'Mr Henry Irving, to whose attraction as an artist the prosperity of the theatre is entirely attributable'.[7] There was, in fact, a growing discrepancy between star and setting. The Bateman management had been marked by rigid economy — the production of *Hamlet* in 1874 which ran for a record 200 performances is alleged to have cost £100 to mount,[8] although the bulk of the expense was undoubtedly concealed in salaries, stock scenery and costumes. But if the Bateman regime denied Irving the support he deserved and the standard of presentation a leading theatre should offer, it nevertheless established the Irving repertoire, a mixture of Shakespearean tragedy with Romantic drama old and new. The comparison with European Romantic drama is perhaps more sobering than helpful. The Lyceum bills did not draw on Hugo or Dumas (except at second-hand in *The Corsican Brothers*), and their nearest approach to French Romantic drama was with Delavigne's *Louis XI*, revived in Boucicault's adaptation originally made for Charles Kean. Irving was more at home with the out-and-out melodrama of *The Bells* and *The Lyons Mail* or the French themes of *Richelieu* and *The Lady of Lyons* purveyed for Macready by Bulwer-Lytton. His borrowing from German Romantic drama was even freer: the short-lived *Vanderdecken* harked back to Fitzball, not Wagner, and the adaptation of *Faust* which W.G. Wills was to provide owed more to Gounod than Goethe. Irving's years at the Lyceum marked the triumph of the Romantic movement in the English theatre, but it was a triumph to which the Romantic writers contributed little, unless Tennyson is counted in their number. Even the English novelists who had been plundered by earlier actors were largely ignored: Scott's work supplied only *Ravenswood,* and Dickens's *Tale of Two Cities* was rejected in favour of *The Dead Heart* (thus leaving Martin Harvey clear to achieve fame with *The Only Way*).

The four Shakespearean roles Irving played under the Batemans (and which he was to repeat, amongst others, during his own management) were Hamlet, Macbeth, Othello, and Richard III. Of these, his Hamlet was outstandingly the most successful. Indeed if Irving's triumph in *The Bells* saved Bateman from bankruptcy, it was *Hamlet* three years later which established the Lyceum as London's leading theatre, and his success in this part enabled him to survive partial failure (as Macbeth) or worse (Othello). For the actor at that stage of his career (he was thirty-six) the role of Hamlet was not only supremely testing but supremely suited. The meditative mood and leisured tempo of the soliloquies summoned up his greatest strength, concentrated intelligence and haunting beauty, and skirted round the effects his limited powers could not provide. Clement Scott repeatedly drew attention to Irving's fulfilment of Hazlitt's call for 'a Hamlet who thinks aloud', and to audiences accustomed to the declamation of Barry Sullivan (or less worthy interpreters) such introspection must have proved a revelation. In addition, although sustained passion was beyond him, he could rise to moments of sudden frenzy when voicing his frustrated love for Ophelia or after the play-scene hurling himself into the throne Claudius had just vacated. When Irving chose *Hamlet* to inaugurate his own management of the Lyceum, with Ellen Terry adding poignancy to the romantic strain in the play, he was able to emphasise these scenes at the expense of the Renaissance revenge theme which stretched beyond his range.

In 1876 when Irving first played Macbeth, a playgoer summed him up as 'a sort of degenerate brother to Hamlet',[9] a comparison enhancing his achievement as the Prince of Denmark, while defining his limitations as the Thane of Cawdor. His own production, twelve years later, met with a similarly controversial response, though his Lady Macbeth was now the highly sensitive Ellen Terry, who saw in him 'a great famished wolf',[10] and the production was impressive visually (Hawes Craven) and musically (Arthur Sullivan). It may be noted that remorse is the dominant note of Mathias and Eugene

Scenes from Irving's production of *Hamlet*, originally staged in 1878. Above Act I: Scene 2; below Act V: Scene 1. Pen-and-ink sketches by Marion Clarkson.

Aram, and in such parts Irving was uniquely and consistently triumphant, but remorse is only a constituent element in the make-up of Macbeth. The critic of the *Pall Mall Gazette* pin-pointed the merits and faults of Irving's performance in a reference to his handling of the 'Dagger Soliloquy':

> Down to 'There's no such thing' his delivery is full of originality
> and power, his sidelong glance at the visionary weapon being
> wonderfully telling; but from 'Now o'er the one half world' he is
> ineffective . . .[11]

clearly confirming that his strength was visual and his weakness vocal.

Under the Bateman management *Othello* offered Irving as the Moor in a performance that reached its high point with the speech before the Senate. There were four acts to follow. When he staged the play himself in 1881, he alternated the parts of Othello and Iago with Edwin Booth, who had been struggling against public indifference in a season at the Princess's. The gesture was at once generous and shrewd, for a London audience which had recently witnessed Salvini's immensely strong Othello was unlikely to accept Irving's, and his reception, not merely by the press, was as dismissive as ever. 'I could not bear to see him in the part. It was painful to me,' wrote his new Desdemona.[12] On the other hand, as Iago he conquered press and public by his subtlety, whereas Booth's was in Ellen Terry's view 'deadly commonplace . . . he showed the villain in all the scenes'. In Iago, as in Iachimo fifteen years later, Irving could draw on his gift for the strangely sinister to provide a Shakespearean performance wholly within his range. In particular, there was a paean of praise for his treatment of the scene in which Iago stood apart, watching Cassio's attentions to Desdemona. He marked his contempt for such folly by eating grapes and spitting out the seeds 'as if each one represented a worthy virtue to be put out of one's mouth'[13] in Ellen Terry's words. *Punch* seized on this scene for a comic comparison between Lyceum Shakespeare and Drury Lane pantomime:

> Mr Irving showed himself not only a great Comedian, but also
> in his stage-management a master of pantomime business,

16

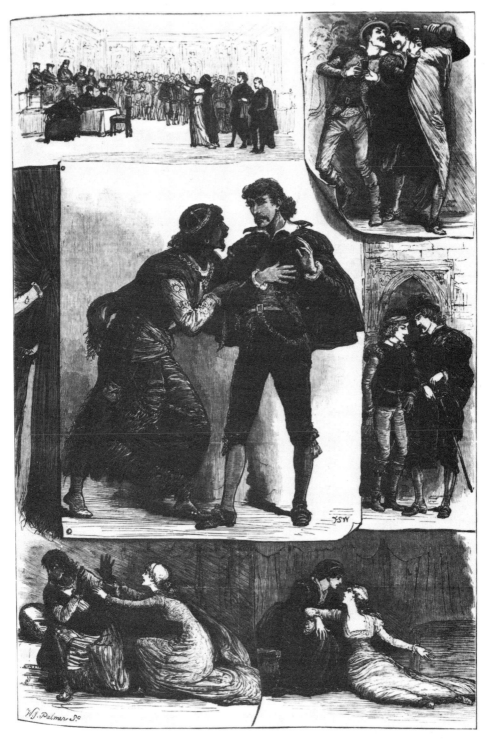

Scenes from Irving's production of *Othello*, 1881. Among those pictured are Irving
as Iago (by 'F.S.W.'), Edwin Booth as Othello, Ellen Terry as Desdemona, William
Terriss as Cassio, A.W. Pinero as Roderigo, and Miss Pauncefort as Emilia.

though we are still doubtful whether the butter-slide, the red-hot poker, and the traditional exchanges of the clown·and the shopkeeper, i.e. when the clown lies down at the threshold of the shop so that the unwary tradesman should first tumble over him and then be whacked when prostrate, might not have been judiciously introduced.[14]

The man who could triumph as Iago might be expected to succeed as Richard III, and to some degree Irving in the early production (1877) did so. The blackly comic wooing of Lady Anne showed off his command of irony, and the tent scene drew deep on his haunted vein (Mathias on the eve of Bosworth Field). But the battle scenes predictably proved beyond him, as his desperate recourse of biting the victorious Richmond's sword (evidently an extension of Edmund Kean's gesture in trying to grasp it) indicates. His Crookback had many admirers, but it may be deduced that Irving himself was not of their number, for he allowed the part to drop out of his repertory for twenty years. When he returned to Richard in 1896 he was approaching sixty, and the already risky venture was wrecked by the injury he sustained immediately after the first night. A curiously parallel fate had attended his production of *King Lear* four years earlier; not a fall, but a disastrous decision to use an 'old man's' voice which made his delivery even slower and stranger than his critics had always alleged. Yet he could and did captivate his audience as Louis XI, another senescent monarch, giving his last performance two nights before his death.

The cast of his earlier *Richard III* included both the Bateman daughters: Isabel as Lady Anne and Kate as Queen Margaret. It also proved to be Irving's last Shakespearean production under the Bateman management. Since the death of Colonel Bateman during the run of *Hamlet*, his widow had depended increasingly on Irving in her running of the Lyceum. Irving, on the other hand, had made himself increasingly independent of the Batemans as he advanced in popularity and prestige. The time had come for him to command the Lyceum in principle as well as practice, and due to the tact and sense of Mrs Bateman this change was amicably achieved in the summer of 1878, when Irving took over the lease. The changes in personnel he made were by no means sweeping: of the three aides on whom his reign at the Lyceum was to depend, two — Hawes Craven, his designer-in-chief, and H.J. Loveday, his stage-manager — already held those posts, while the third, Bram Stoker, shortly took over as company manager. But there was one change which both he and Mrs Bateman knew the take-over rendered inevitable. Isabel Bateman moved to Sadler's Wells, of which her mother had bravely if rashly taken a lease. Irving was thus free to offer the position of leading lady to the actress who had recently enchanted the London public in *Olivia* at the Court.

The contribution made by Ellen Terry to Irving's management of the Lyceum is easy to record, but much more difficult to assess. From the opening of *Hamlet* in December 1878 to the opening of *Coriolanus* in April 1901, she retained her status, and even after that date she rejoined Irving for provincial tours. When the main item on the bill offered her no suitable role (as in *The Bells* or *Louis XI*, for instance), she regularly appeared in a short piece tailored to her measure, such as *Nance Oldfield* or *The Amber Heart*. Her admirers, more numerous and expressive than Irving's, often accused him of under-using her, for example in *Eugene Aram* and several of the later Lyceum productions such as *Robespierre* or *The Medicine Man*. She herself felt that she lost the chance of playing Rosalind because he would not tackle Jacques and could not play Orlando.

On the other hand, she loyally pointed out that several productions gave her finer opportunities than him (particularly *The Cup, Olivia,* and *Cymbeline*), and that in *The Merchant of Venice, Macbeth, Much Ado About Nothing,* and *Henry VIII,* her success was commensurate with his, in some instances greater. Their partnership was shrewdly planned and successfully employed. Not only did she exercise the kind of personal fascination beyond the powers of an actor or less enchanting actress; she brought to the Lyceum a wealth of experience from a stage career begun before she could walk, whereas Irving was a late starter and by no means a born performer. His estimate of her importance to the box office is already evident from the salary list of 1881 in which the leading lady rates £200 a week. Irving allowed himself £60. The next highest paid performer (William Terriss, a star in his own right) receives £20.[15]

The compatability of their acting styles is equally significant, though less well documented. Ellen Terry was fond of describing herself as a 'useful' actress, but she could hardly be described as versatile, in that tragedy did not lie easily within her range, and her Juliet, Lady Macbeth, and Volumnia were widely criticised. It is

19

significant that her most successful appearances in Shakespearean tragedy were as Ophelia, Desdemona, and Cordelia — all relatively brief roles. Her fiercest critic was undoubtedly Henry James. Even before she joined Irving he expressed reservations about her gifts: 'She is intelligent and vivacious . . . but she has, with them, the defect that she is simply *not* an actress'; with Irving he found her 'aesthetic' but 'amateurish' (in *The Lady of Lyons*); 'too free and familiar' as Portia; 'not a Juliet'; 'rough' as Margaret in *Faust*; and only really acceptable as Imogen.[16] He was, of course, comparing her unfavourably with the leading ladies of the Comédie Française, whose rigorously trained talents defined for him the comédienne. Most of Ellen Terry's admirers, meaning not only the crowds who thronged the Lyceum but at various times Charles Reade, Tom Taylor, Edward Godwin, Lewis Carroll, and Oscar Wilde, would have protested that it was precisely because she did not conform to the genre of comédienne that they loved her, pointing perhaps to other English actresses (including her sisters, Kate and Marion) who did so conform but did not inspire such devotion. It may be recalled that Shaw carried his worship to the extreme of writing her 250 letters and three leading roles (Candida, The Strange Lady, Cicely Wayneflete) before he even met her.

The actress herself knew that her two great gifts were speed and sympathy. She liked to quote as her motto Beatrice's 'There was a star danced; and under that was I born', and her failing memory retained Portia's speech on mercy to the end of her career. At the Lyceum her turn of speed was often checked; Portia (in the Trial Scene), Juliet, and Beatrice were three parts in which she had reluctantly to accept Irving's tempo instead of her own. But these gifts were enhanced by a quality of directness, of immediate and overwhelming appeal to the audience which was at once physical and spiritual, and which complemented exactly Irving's aura of mystery and often deviousness. Thus even with a text as pedestrian as Wills's *Faust* the simplicity and grace of her Margaret proved irresistible. Indeed, outside Shakespeare she was often more successful in the commonplace than the accomplished, triumphing as Olivia, the vicar's daughter, but cramped and confined in Ibsen (as Hjördis in *The Vikings*), Barrie (in *Alice-Sit-By-The-Fire*, an unhappy title for the child of a dancing star), or even Shaw. In one of the lectures she gave in later years she defined her approach:

An actress does not study a character with a view to proving
something about the dramatist who created it. Her task is to
learn how to translate this character into herself, how to make its
thoughts, her thoughts, its words her words.[17]

The comment explains both her few failures and her many successes.

The enduring success of the partnership was undoubtedly *The
Merchant of Venice.* It followed on the heels of *Hamlet* after Irving
had taken over the Lyceum, and he was still playing Shylock in that
last fatal week at Bradford more than a quarter of a century later. For
Irving this was to a large extent a matter of physical suitability; the
man who first played Jessica's father at forty-one could still plausibly
claim that relationship at sixty-seven. But there was much more to
Irving's success as Shylock than convincing appearance. The play
itself came nearer to Romantic melodrama than any other Lyceum
Shakespeare (though *Cymbeline* was to press it hard). A Victorian
playwright might easily have tackled the theme of the heroine in
male disguise pleading for the hero's life, though he would surely
have amalgamated the roles of Bassanio and Antonio, and arranged
that the crucial bond had been signed to save the credit of the
heroine's father. Even more exact was Shylock's correspondence to
the Victorian villain as Irving uniquely portrayed him: powerful yet
vulnerable (Mathias, Louis XI); proudly paternal (Lesurques,
Dr Primrose); devious yet dignified (Philip II, Digby Grant). *The
Merchant of Venice* displayed Irving and Terry at their keenest pitch;
they knew it and kept the parts sharp and shining.

This sustained success was closely approached by that of *Much
Ado about Nothing,* and it was doubtless only the inexorability of the
years which prevented their Benedick and Beatrice from holding the
stage as long as Shylock and Portia. Benedick was Irving's only
successful essay in Shakespearean comedy, and his popularity in this
role contrasts interestingly with his failure in *Twelfth Night,* an
unhappy play in the Lyceum canon, since not only did the Malvolio
disappoint, but the niceties of Sir Toby and Sir Andrew proved
beyond the comic range of Irving's stock clowns; Orsino was totally
alien to the extrovert style of William Terriss, and even Ellen Terry
fell short of Viola's measure on the first night, due apparently to a
poisoned finger, which weakened her whole performance. *Much
Ado,* however, became as much melodrama as comedy; it is no

21

Irving and Ellen Terry in Act IV of *The Merchant of Venice*, originally staged in 1879. Pen-and-ink sketch by Marion Clarkson.

coincidence that the best recorded features of the production were Terry's radiant Beatrice and the Church Scene, reverently preserved in a painting by the Claudio, Johnston Forbes-Robertson. Even more significant than the monumental impression achieved by Telbin, the designer, in this scene, was Irving's insistence on retaining the conventional 'false' ending. Beatrice's 'Kill Claudio' produces (after some persuasion) a satisfactory response from Benedick: 'Enough. I am engaged: I will challenge him', and the serviceable exit line: 'Go comfort your cousin: I must say she is dead; and so farewell'. But this was not 'enough' for Victorian actor-managers, and these spurious lines were regularly added:

BEATRICE: Benedick, kill him — kill him, if you can.
BENEDICK: As sure as I'm alive, I will!

By emphasising the swashbuckler in Benedick, Irving was able to conceal his lack of self-mockery, a lack which sadly handicapped his Malvolio.

Benedick is a late and reluctant lover, and this aspect of the character suited Irving admirably. For precisely the opposite reason his Romeo the year before was a failure (though his *Romeo and Juliet* was a considerable box-office success). The criticism that he (at forty-four) and Ellen Terry (at thirty-five) were both too old is only partly relevant — successful Romeos and Juliets must by definition be too old for these roles. Much more serious was Irving's lack of youthful feeling, not only in his voice but in his whole approach. All the vocal peculiarities his critics fastened on handicapped him as a young lover. Henry Arthur Jones's comment — 'He could not untwist the chains that tie the hidden soul of harmony . . . It would be difficult to recall any one sustained passage of Shakespeare's verse that was spoken by Irving in such a way as to delight or even to satisfy the ear as well as the mind'[18] — applies with especial force to this performance. Ellen Terry, who had responded feelingly to Irving's conception of Hamlet as the blighted lover, recorded his failure as Romeo in the Friar's cell scene: 'He screamed, grew slower and slower, and looked older and older', because the 'actor of commoner mould', as she knew from a wealth of experience,

takes such scenes rhetorically — recites them, and gets through them with some success. But the actor who impersonates, feels,

and lives such anguish or passion or tempestuous grief, does for
the moment in imagination nearly die. Imagination impeded
Henry Irving in what are known as 'strong' scenes.[19]

Irving's success in Shakespeare during his later years seemed
inversely proportionate to the worth of the plays themselves. His
Lear, as has been seen, was felled by first-night nerves and
miscalculation. His Coriolanus had been planned for twenty years; it
was probably outside his capacities in 1880, and was manifestly
beyond him by 1901. On the other hand, Iachimo gave him an
opportunity to repeat his triumph as Iago (and to enlarge the part
by reducing the importance of Posthumus), while the undoubted
triumph of his final years was as Wolsey in a play Shakespeare
helped to write. Many observers, both during and after his lifetime,
commented that Irving with his fine face and bearing would have
made a splendid statesman or leader of the church. During the run of
*Henry VIII* it was reported that the dignity and distinction of
Irving's Cardinal 'induced several unbelievers of long standing to
conversion and penitence',[20] a statement that prompts the question:
From what heresies to what beliefs? Monarchism to distrust of
princes? Founding Oxford colleges to life insurance? The comment
of Sir Robert Peel to Irving: 'Your Grace just looked what
Wilberforce once said of Manning, "the very incarnation of evil" ',
though gravely unjust to both Cardinals, tallies more closely with
the picture Irving presented of Wolsey.[21]

Outside Shakespeare his greatest successes in the last twenty years
were *Faust* and *Becket*. The two plays, and his performances as
Mephistopheles and Becket, are not only complementary but
represent his range as an actor: the diptych of demon and saint,
Dubosc and Lesurques, Mathias the murderer and Mathias the
burgomaster, Louis XI the king and Louis XI the coward. Both texts
were the result of lengthy and large-scale preparation. In each case
Irving took a monumental work by a philosopher-poet and carved
out of it a much simplified dramatic narrative, based on striking
pictorial effects and strong contrasts of character. Neither Goethe's
nor Tennyson's achievement was adequately represented: the
Lyceum *Faust* consisted of a heavily cut version of Goethe's Part I,
while according to Bram Stoker's evidence only five-sevenths of the
published text of *Becket* found its way into the acting version.[22] On

Irving as Mephistopheles in *Faust*, 1885.
Original water-colour in the Garrick Club.

the other hand, a full performance of either work would undoubtedly have defeated both actors and audience, and by this summary treatment Irving provided his public with a satisfying if fragmentary insight into two singularly intractable dramas.

Irving planned his production of *Faust* for five years, first commissioning an anonymous 'treatment' of John Anster's early nineteenth-century translation, and then entrusting the suggestible W.G. Wills with the acting version. These protracted and elaborate preparations resulted in probably the most spectacular triumph of his management: the total cost of staging *Faust* has been calculated as £15,402 (compared with £1,100 for the 1878 *Hamlet*), but the public paid £69,447 to see it during the season 1885—86 and £57,016 the following year,[23] while the production was a powerful attraction on two American tours, enormously popular in the provinces, and was several times revived. Irving continued to build up its pictorial impact during the original run — the Witches' Kitchen scene, for example, was not added until the 244th performance — and several of the tableaux presented in this play exceeded all his previous achievements, above all the Walpurgisnacht revels on the Brocken Mountain, which employed an acting company and stage staff some 350 strong, an orchestra of nearly 40, and an off-stage chorus of 43.[24] Irving's own performance as Mephistopheles was itself greatly enhanced by visual effects — his scarlet robes consistently pinpointed against the subdued tones of the scenery and other costumes; his important exits and entrances effected in clouds of steam; his face illuminated at crucial moments by battery-operated lights in his cap.

All this suggests more the pantomime demon than the spokesman of Satan, and yet the numerous comparisons made between Irving's Mephistopheles and Milton's Lucifer emphasise how far above pantomime Irving raised the play at this point. As always, there was a strong glint of grim comedy in this portrayal of evil. His comment on Margaret's garrulous neighbour, Martha — 'Where will she go to, by and by, I wonder? I won't have her' — was singled out by press and public as a masterstroke of comic acting wherever the play was performed. Ellen Terry had little assistance from Wills's text in her portrayal of Margaret, the simple, trusting girl, but against all odds (including her age — she was nearly thirty-eight when she created the part, and continued to play it for ten years) she presented a figure both plausible and sympathetic. *Faust*, even more than Irving's

The Witches' Kitchen (Act I: Scene 2) from *Faust*. Sketch by Gerard Hopkins, showing Irving as Mephistopheles and George Alexander as Faust. This scene was added on 15 November 1886.

successful Shakespearean productions, epitomises his gifts as actor
and director. He was wholly in control of his material and the result
on its own terms was unsurpassable.

*Becket* was even longer in preparation than *Faust*, and Irving's
association with Tennyson dated back twenty years to the production
of *Queen Mary*. This piece, put up as a platform for the Bateman
family (Kate appeared in the title role, Isabel and a third sister,
Virginia, supported her) hardly fulfilled their or the author's
expectations. Irving's designated part, Cardinal Pole, was cut
completely, and he found himself translated to Philip of Spain,
making only two brief appearances which nevertheless remained in
the public's memory when the play had faded. Tennyson himself
commented drily: 'Strange thing about Philip, I didn't know I'd
written it',[25] and Whistler's portrait immortalised the actor's
interpretation of the cold, calculating king. Now that he was licensee
of the Lyceum, Irving set about coaxing another play from the Poet
Laureate. Of the various figures discussed (King Arthur, Don
Quixote, Robin Hood), Becket appealed most to Tennyson, and in
1879 he handed over a manuscript so voluminous that for a long
time both Irving and Bram Stoker lacked the courage to untie the
parcel.[26]

complete, but meanwhile the Lyceum had successfully staged
Tennyson's short play, *The Cup*. It was notable chiefly for the stage
picture presented by the Temple of Artemis in Act II, and for Ellen
Terry's portrayal of the High Priestess, Camma, offering the
poisoned marriage cup to Irving as Synorix, her husband's murderer.
Consultations on *Becket* followed the publication of the play in 1884.
Finally, with Tennyson nearing his end, responsibility was handed
over to the actor, the poet himself declaring: 'I can trust Irving — he
will do me justice',[27] and *Becket* was first performed in February
1893, four months after Tennyson's death.

If Irving did not do justice to the whole work, he wrought from it a
series of impressive tableaux, and a part that suited his 'saintly' style
unreservedly. Critics noted that he had played three princes of the
church: Richelieu, Wolsey, and Becket — and the last had the
unmistakable stamp of greatness, both as statesman (denouncing
the king's 'customs' in the council at Northampton Castle) and
martyr:

On a Tuesday was I born . . .
On a Tuesday from mine exile I return'd,
And on a Tuesday —

(*Tracy enters, then Fitzurse, De Brito, and De Morville. Monks following.*)

                — on a Tuesday — Tracy!

(*A long silence, broken by Fitzurse saying, contemptuously*)

God help thee!

The cuts and transpositions Irving made in Tennyson's text greatly reduced the historical argument and advanced the romantic figure of Fair Rosamund in her Bower (occupying the whole of the Lyceum stage in Hawes Craven's lavish setting). The poet had himself contrived to link the characters of Rosamund and Becket, notably in the confrontation between Queen Eleanor and her rival, by bringing Becket to the rescue with all the panache of an Adelphi melodrama:

ELEANOR (*raising the dagger*): This in thy bosom, fool,
      And after in thy bastard's!

(*Enter Becket from behind. Catches hold of her arm.*)

BECKET: Murderess!

In the last act Tennyson also arranged for Rosamund to appear in Canterbury Cathedral in time for the Archbishop's murder, though with no reciprocal benefit save for Ellen Terry's participation in the final tableau. The Lyceum audiences relished both scenes, however, and when *Becket* was played at Windsor Castle a month later, Queen Victoria endorsed their verdict: 'The last scene, where Becket refuses to fly and defies his murderers is very fine, and his death and the way he falls down the steps very striking.'[28] Her approval eased the way to the knighthood conferred on Irving two years later.

*Becket* stayed in the actor's repertoire and was his last solid success. His increasingly desperate search for suitable roles was due in large measure to the difficulty of accommodating both himself and Ellen Terry in their maturity, but another difficulty was the maturing of English drama itself. The 1890s saw the emergence of English playwrights practised in Society drama — 'problem plays' set in elegant Mayfair drawing-rooms and written by architects of sound dramatic construction like Pinero (a graduate of the Lyceum Academy) or sophisticated entertainers like Oscar Wilde. Irving's roots, however, lay wholly in Romantic drama; it was not merely that he rejected Ibsen (his audience was just as resistant to such an unpalatable diet), but that he could not adjust to contemporary comedy or drama, as *The Medicine Man* unhappily proved.

Hence arose his blind reliance on old hands like Wills, Comyns Carr, or the capable Conan Doyle, to provide him with romantic scenarios like *Don Quixote, King Arthur,* and *A Story of Waterloo,* the last contemporary in setting but suffused with nostalgia for a glorious past: 'The Guards want powder; and, by God, the Guards shall have it!' In the end he despaired of English drama altogether and turned exclusively to the French school, playing Napoleon to Ellen Terry's Madame Sans-Gêne and commissioning *Robespierre* and *Dante* from the increasingly outmoded Sardou. He even negotiated for the English rights of *Cyrano de Bergerac* before admitting defeat and relinquishing the play to Tree and ultimately Wyndham.[29]

*Becket,* however, held his and the public's affection. Indeed, as disaster began to assail him — the destruction by fire of his scenic store in 1898; the loss of control over the Lyceum; ultimately the surrender of his tenancy, together with failing strength — the role of the martyred high priest seemed to acquire an added poignancy in his audience's eyes. After seeing him in the part on tour, the author and actress, Naomi Jacob, found the real thing second-rate:

> Speaking to my mother one day about various dignitaries of the Church, I said: 'They're always faintly disappointing in real life, aren't they?'
> 'Yes', she replied. 'You see, you saw Irving as Becket — '

Her neighbour in the gallery that night had psychic powers:

> He fell, and a stout lady next to me, who might have been some small shopkeeper, hissed: 'Gawd, the — — — —s 'ave murdered 'im!'[30]

It is hard to believe that his final appearance and last words on the stage — 'Into Thy hands, O Lord — into Thy hands' — spoken less

'Rosamund's Bower' (Act III: Scene 3) from *Becket*, 1893, showing Irving as Becket, Ellen Terry as Rosamund de Clifford, and Geneviève Ward as Queen Eleanor. Water-colour by Arthur Jole Goodman.

than an hour before his death, were not somehow divinely ordained — or stage-managed. For an artist as dedicated as Irving the two interpretations are fused.

It has been suggested that, although acknowledged leader of his profession for more than thirty years, Irving's acting was subjected to more ridicule and his fame more often impugned than any comparable performer before or since. This controversy, however, was by no means a check to Irving's increasing pre-eminence. As the entertainment world continues to demonstrate, an allegedly inflated reputation can sometimes justify itself more resoundingly than solid worth. Irving's detractors, perhaps unwittingly, did him considerable service by provoking others to see and judge him. Even they themselves could not afford to ignore him.

One of the most insistent charges levelled against him and one still current argues that the entire resources of the Lyceum were deployed to enhance his performance, and some contemporary critics like Shaw implied that this tactic, permissible for a barn-stormer such as Gustavus Vaughan Brooke or Barry Sullivan, was unforgiveable in the master of London's leading theatre. Where the charge refers to the melodramas in his repertoire, it betrays a misunderstanding of the actor-manager's stage. As in the operatic repertoire, many plays of the period were conceived as vehicles for the extraordinary powers of a proven performer, the supporting parts being filled in as lines of business which called for loyal and disciplined playing but no especially individual talent. Of Irving's stand-bys *The Bells, The Lyons Mail,* and *Louis XI,* all lacked a female lead worthy of Ellen Terry's gifts, but Gordon Craig stresses the importance to Irving of John Archer as the Mesmerist in *The Bells* and Fouinard in *The Lyons Mail* (both small parts but crucially important in key-scenes),[31] and Irving coaxed William Terriss back from his starring roles at the Adelphi to play Nemours, on whose mercy the King throws himself in the turning-point of *Louis XI.*

When assessing Irving's Shakespearean or comparable productions, it is often difficult to distinguish between his work as actor and producer. The pains he took to maintain and extend the prestige of the Lyceum resulted in an ensemble far removed from the efforts of Macready, for example, who was working under decidedly adverse conditions, or Charles Kean, equally dedicated but less inspired or inspiring. The often protracted gestation of a Lyceum production

Four cartoons in silhouette of Irving as Louis XI, 1878.

(twenty years for *Coriolanus,* fourteen for *Becket*) tended to obscure Irving's priorities. But there was never any doubt in the minds of Irving's staff that the 'Guv'nor's' performance took precedence. Ellen Terry learnt that lesson early. In her first appearance at the Lyceum she planned to use her understanding of costume (largely derived from her training by E.W. Godwin) to her own advantage:

'In the first scene I wear a pinkish dress. It's all rose-coloured with her. Her father and brother love her. The Prince loves her — and so she wears pink.'

'Pink,' repeated Henry thoughtfully.

'In the nunnery scene I have a pale, gold, amber dress — the most beautiful colour. The material is a church brocade. It will "tone down" the colour of my hair. In the last scene I wear a transparent, black dress.'

Henry did not wag an eyelid.

'I see. In mourning for her father.'

'No, not exactly that. I think *red* was the mourning colour of the period. But black seems to me *right* — like the character, like the situation.'

'Would you put the dresses on?' said Henry gravely.

At that minute Walter Lacy came up, that very Walter Lacy who had been with Charles Kean when I was a child, and who now acted as adviser to Henry Irving in his Shakespearean productions.

'Ah, here's Lacy. Would you mind, Miss Terry, telling Mr Lacy what you are going to wear?'

Rather surprised, but still unsuspecting, I told Lacy all over again. Pink in the first scene, yellow in the second, black —

You should have seen Lacy's face at the word 'black'. He was going to burst out, but Henry stopped him. He was more diplomatic than that!

'Ophelias generally wear *white,* don't they?'

'I believe so,' I answered, 'but black is more interesting.'

'I should have thought you would look much better in white.'

'Oh, no!' I said.

And then they dropped the subject for that day. It *was* clever of him!

The next day Lacy came up to me:

'You didn't really mean that you are going to wear black in the mad scene?'

'Yes, I did. Why not?'

'*Why not!* My God! Madam, there must be only one black
figure in this play, and that's Hamlet!'[32]

But if she had thus to learn to 'give', she also learnt how meticulous
her manager could be about his staff supporting not only his efforts
but also his leading lady's. Conditioned both by her life with Godwin
and by service under the Bancrofts and their pupil, John Hare, to
extensive and rigorous rehearsal, she grew fretful at Irving's apparent
neglect where her scenes were concerned:

> I was still a stranger in the theatre, and in awe of Henry Irving
> personally; but I plucked up courage, and said:
> 'I am very nervous about my first appearance with you.
> Couldn't we rehearse *our* scenes?'
> '*We* shall be all right,' he answered, 'but we are not going to
> run the risk of being bottled up by a gas-man or a fiddler.'[33]

His dedication was total, and extended beyond the long years of
preparation to the actual rehearsals, which could stretch over eight
to ten weeks, and in the final phase last from 10 a.m. to the small
hours of the following day. 'Last night was a desperate affair' wrote
Irving to Ellen Terry of a *Faust* rehearsal, 'from seven till five this
morning. Then only to end of 3rd act.'[34] At the same time he could
be swift and summary when necessary. The elaborate scene prepared
by William Telbin for Margaret's transfiguration, complete with
angels and rainbow, was scrapped at the dress rehearsal and replaced
by a simple blue background of Irving's devising.[35] Alfred Thompson
was commissioned to design the costumes for *Romeo and Juliet,* but
when his work was completed Irving decided they would be
ineffective theatrically, and instructed the wardrobe staff to copy
illustrations from sources of his own providing.[36] The scenery for
*Macbeth* was entrusted, appropriately enough, to an associate of the
Royal Scottish Academy, Keeley Halsewelle, who proved incapable
of converting his sketches into scenic paint and had to be replaced by
the tried team of Hawes Craven and Company.[37] Nor was Irving's
mastery of detail reserved for the 'big' occasion; Ellen Terry testifies
that he was as scrupulous in supervising a single matinee of *Werner,*
staged for charity, as over his spectacular productions of Shakespeare
or *Faust.*[38]

In the course of his twenty-five years as lord of the Lyceum,

Irving refined and reconciled the guiding principles which had informed Shakespearean production throughout the nineteenth century: the staging of the plays as a sequence of striking pictures, based on historical or pseudo-historical evidence, intended to entertain and educate the audience at the same time. It was to these objectives that the Kembles had directed their management at Covent Garden, as had Macready during his brief tenure of first Covent Garden and then Drury Lane. Clearly the emphasis could be changed: Charles Kean, perhaps more zealous as archaeologist than actor, declared that his work at the Princess's had been planned 'that historical accuracy might be so blended with pictorial effect that instruction and amusement might go hand in hand. . . . In fact I was anxious to make the theatre a school as well as a recreation'.[39]

Irving took a more balanced view. Though never a scholar, he recognised the theatrical significance of scholarship. Before tackling Shylock he took his production team to Venice; to play Wolsey he had his Cardinal's robes sent to Rome to be dyed; E.W. Godwin was consulted on the designs for *The Cup*, Alma Tadema on *Henry VIII* and *Coriolanus*. His editions of the plays, published as they were produced, demonstrated the seriousness of his study, if not always its thoroughness. But scholarship was never an end in itself for him, as it could be with Charles Kean. Ellen Terry observed that when preparing *Madame Sans-Gêne* he filled his rooms at Grafton Street with Napoleonic material, but 'It was not *Napoleon* who interested Henry Irving, but *Napoleon for his purpose,* two very different things'.[40] In fact the 'authentic' Roman dye on Wolsey's robes was found to take stage-light poorly, and the garment had to be remade in the Lyceum wardrobe.[41]

Irving saw accuracy in production as an aid to effect. At a time when scholars had yet to examine and reassess the resources of the Elizabethan stage, he could be surprisingly far-sighted, asserting that 'Shakespeare if well acted on a bare stage would certainly afford great intellectual pleasure', but he would not have been the most famous actor-manager of the century had he not added: 'that pleasure will be all the greater if the eye be charmed, at the same time, by scenic illustrations in harmony with the poet's ideas'.[42] In an interview he gave to the *Pall Mall Gazette* during the triumphant run of *Faust*, he stated his belief that 'the first duty of any one who mounts a piece is to provide a beautiful and pleasing effect' and to this end 'archaeology must give way to beauty'.[43] In fact his designers had based their work for *Faust* on Nüremberg, not Dresden as Goethe called for. Nüremberg was more picturesque.

Irving's progress to the summit of pictorial theatre was gradual: *Hamlet, The Merchant of Venice,* and *Othello* were ably but modestly mounted. A watershed in the course of Lyceum Shakespeare seems to have been the visit to Drury Lane in 1881 of the Meiningen Company with their masterly ensemble — a permanent company supporting guest principals. Ellen Terry says of their next production, *Romeo and Juliet*: 'It was the most *elaborate* of all the Lyceum productions. In it Henry first displayed his mastery of crowds', and gives a revealing insight into Irving's reasoning: 'Henry once said to me *Hamlet* could be played anywhere on its acting merits. It marches from situation to situation. But *Romeo* proceeds from picture to picture.'[44] Perhaps, too, he realised that with both the leading roles less than perfectly cast, pictorial and crowd effects were acutely needed, as the box-office confirmed. In any case, his feet were firmly planted on the path of spectacular Shakespeare.

To achieve this spectacle he had at his disposal the system of set scenes with which his predecessors had gradually replaced conventional Georgian staging (using flats in fixed positions determined by the grooves, visual scene-changes, and adherence to a single acting level, necessitated by the grooves themselves). The specially 'set' scene, which has bequeathed its name to scenery of every description, used scenic features of varying shapes and size, braced at any required angle, in front of elaborate backcloths and ultimately the illuminated cyclorama. Many of the elements were three-dimensional, and different acting levels composed of platforms and steps could now be employed. The principle of providing appropriate scenery and costumes for every play, fostered by Macready and cherished by Charles Kean, became a guiding line of Irving's policy. To achieve his end, he had amongst his designers Hawes Craven, inherited from the Bateman regime, William L. Telbin, descended from the family which had worked for many leading Victorian actors, and later Joseph Harker, who was to carry the standard of Lyceum scenic splendour well into the twentieth century.

Following *Romeo and Juliet*, therefore, each Shakespearean revival was hailed for at least one magnificent evocation of a past age: in *Much Ado* the monumental interior of Messina Cathedral with pillars 30 feet high; in *Macbeth* the arched and galleried Banqueting Hall; in *Henry VIII* Wolsey's feast at York Place with its myriads of Masquers stepping to the strains that have lingered ever since in Edward German's Three Dances; in *Lear* Dover Cliffs used as a background throughout the last act; in *Coriolanus* Alma Tadema's painstaking reconstruction of the Capitol. Occasionally voices were raised in protest against the elaboration of scenic effects: 'The more Shakespeare is built in, the more we are built out' was Henry James's comment,[45] but the public revelled in the spectacle. From *Faust* and *Macbeth* onwards a souvenir of each major production was published, the illustrations often contributed by the designers themselves, an interesting extension of the records Charles Kean commissioned for his own satisfaction.

As with Irving's predecessors and successors, the cost of these stunning *coups du théâtre* was sometimes lengthy waits and intervals. The Cathedral scene in *Much Ado About Nothing* took fifteen minutes to erect,[46] and the St Lorenz Platz in *Faust* twelve minutes.[47] Such delays were not inevitable, however; Percy Fitzgerald testified that only thirty-eight seconds were needed to change a Paris salon in *The Corsican Brothers* to the Forest of Versailles, with real snow (or rather real salt).[48] It would be unjust to Irving's particular flair for stage spectacle to stress the time and effort involved. His aim and to a large extent his achievement were distinct from the architectural precision of his rivals, and consisted essentially in a quality of illusion characterised by the mystery and magic in which he excelled as an actor. The early Victorian theatre with its huge, restless audiences and protracted performances had largely precluded the focus and concentration which stage illusion demands. One of Irving's most significant changes at the Lyceum was to frame the scene in a black 'false proscenium', and complement this isolation of the stage action by blacking out the auditorium (a measure impossible in the earlier period which retained 'half-price' and all the street-market activities of the theatre). The effect was to persuade the Lyceum audience that they were witnesses to 'another world', an impression that contributed enormously to the acceptance of Irving's Lyceum as a Temple of Theatrical Art, in a different category from rival establishments, however popular and successful.

In this achievement of theatrical illusion Irving's use of the fully developed resources of gas-lighting was essential. Coinciding as his career did with the apogee of gas and limelight in the theatre before its literal eclipse by electricity, he exploited to the full its refinement and flexibility, underrated by later generations. Ellen Terry insisted that 'The thick softness of gaslight, with the lovely specks and motes in it, so like *natural* light, gave illusion to many a scene which is now revealed in all its naked trashiness',[49] and although electricity was installed at the Lyceum in the 1890s Irving made little use of it. A pioneer of modern stage-lighting, W. Bridges-Adams, nevertheless recalled that 'with gas footlights before him, an actor was seen through an imperceptible shimmer of warm air which lent him magic; and the electric arc had not the soft lambency of limelight'.[50] It may be judged how important this effect was to Irving's particular repertoire and style, with the emphasis always on illusion and often on mystery and menace, so that his handling of gaslight was as crucial in *The Bells* or *Eugene Aram* as in his Shakespearean productions.

The flexibility of his lighting helped to offset the harmful excesses of 'built in' Shakespeare by effecting the melting of one scene into another so often commented on, and to mitigate the long inter-missions and 'carpenters' scenes' (played before a front-drop while the stage-hands audibly prepared the next 'set' scene). There was also widespread comment, not always favourable, on Irving's partiality for darkness as the most dramatic form of stage-light. *Macbeth* in particular provoked loud protest on this score; Inverness was so shrouded in gloom that Duncan's praise — 'This castle hath a pleasant seat' — appeared ludicrous, and when Malcolm in exile was bathed in sunlight, a patriotic playgoer called out: 'Good old England!'[51]

Irving's emphasis on darkness formed part of his overall prin-ciple of contrast, not merely between darkness and light, but between darkness and colour. The effect of his use of blood-red skies as a battlefield background (in *Lear*, *Richard III*, and *Cymbeline*) has been noted. Henry James compared him to 'a painter who goes in for colour when he cannot depend on his drawing'.[52] But perhaps the most telling comment on his use of colour in stage-lighting comes from Bram Stoker, in an anecdote of the Brocken scene in *Faust*. After one of the final rehearsals he felt profound misgivings:

> It was then, as ever afterwards, a wonderful scene of imagination,
> of grouping, of lighting, of action, and all the rush and
> whirl and triumphant cataclysm of unfettered demoniacal pos-
> session. But it all looked cold and unreal . . .

and so alarmed was he that he urged on Irving the need to prepare another production against *Faust*'s failure. The reaction was considered and characteristic:

> As far as tonight goes you are quite right; but you have not seen
> my dress. I do not want to wear it till I get all the rest correct.
> Then you will see. I have studiously kept as yet all the colour-
> scheme to that grey-green. When my dress of flaming scarlet
> appears among it — and remember that the colour will be
> intensified by that very light — it will bring the whole picture to-
> gether in a way you cannot dream of. Indeed, I can hardly realise it
> myself yet, though I know it will be right. You shall see too how
> Ellen Terry's white dress, and even that red scar across her throat,
> will stand out in the midst of that turmoil of lighting.[53]

He was proved right.

Like his choice of plays, Irving's use of lighting sometimes fostered accusations of exhibitionism. Two favourite instances concern the devil-may-care William Terriss, who spoke out against such treatment. As the villain, Château-Renaud, fighting the final duel with Fabien dei Franchi in *The Corsican Brothers,* he stopped the rehearsal to observe:

> Don't you think, Guv'nor, a few rays of the moon might fall on
> me — it shines equally, ye know, on the just and unjust.[54]

while for his first performance as Nemours in *Louis XI,* before the crucial confrontation, he dared to instruct the limelight man: 'The Guv'nor says you are to put the lime on me.' Afterwards, when sternly rebuked, he replied simply: 'Well, you see, Guv'nor, it was the only chance I had.'[55] In Irving's defence it should be noted that the attention he paid to lighting was not always limited to his own performance: his object when rehearsing *Hamlet* was to avoid both himself and Ellen Terry being 'bottled up by a gas-man or a fiddler'.

Music was a field of which he had no technical knowledge but considerable instinctive flair. Admirably served by two musical directors in succession, Hamilton Clarke and Meredith Ball, he turned for many of his major productions to leading composers: to Julius Benedict for *Romeo and Juliet*, to Arthur Sullivan for *Macbeth* and *King Arthur*, to Charles Villiers Stanford for *Becket*. A characteristic story is told of the march Sullivan had composed for *Macbeth*, on which Irving commented: 'As music it's very fine — but for our purpose it's no good at all.' Asked what would be suitable, 'the actor . . . with a combination of rhythmic pantomime and suggestive hummings, strove to convey his idea of what he needed'.[56] The story reflects as much credit on Sullivan, who responded with an acceptable alternative, as on Irving. No doubt long experience of working with Gilbert, who knew only two tunes, 'one of which was "God Save the Queen" and the other wasn't', stood him in good stead.

The elaborate settings and subtle lighting effects which Irving required were a major item in his salary list. The demands on manpower of his most spectacular scenes were enormous: as has been noted, the Brocken scene in *Faust* involved over 400 people, and for some later productions the overall numbers were even larger. *Robespierre*, one of his last Lyceum plays, called on 355 performers (including 235 'supers') and a stage and administrative staff of 284, 90 of these being 'machinists' or stage-hands and 38 lighting crew.[57] While Irving certainly worked in an era of cheap labour — at the beginning of his regime 'supers' were paid a flat rate of 1/− per performance — the cost of operating the Lyceum continued to mount. Expenditure on the later productions was often spread over long periods, as texts, settings, music, and much else were commissioned, completed, and sometimes discarded. *Henry VIII* proved the costliest at £16,543, *Faust* a close second, at £15,402, *Romeo*, the first of the large-scale productions, £9,554. In the early years the outlay was regularly exceeded by the returns — for the season 1882−83 (with *Much Ado* as the new production) a profit of £15,732 was achieved, but the rising scale on which the productions were mounted took its toll, and by 1896−97 (the season marred by Irving's accident after the first night of *Richard III*) a loss of £9,928 was recorded.[58]

Personal profit was never of the least importance to Irving, who for years paid himself a modest £60 a week. Insofar as he made money, he made it for the Lyceum, including in that word not

'The Seven Ages of Society' by Phil May, 1884. The increasing prominence of actors in Society is reflected in the three central tents, filled with theatrical personalities. Irving and Ellen Terry are seen in the middle of the sketch.

## KEY TO THE CARTOON: THE SEVEN AGES OF SOCIETY.

1. Her Majesty the Queen.
2. Prince George of Wales.
3. Princess Louise of Wales.
4. Prince Edward of Wales.
5. Princess Victoria of Wales.
6. Princess Maud of Wales.
7. Duchess of Connaught.
8. Duke of Connaught.
9. Princess Louise.
10. Marquis of Lorne.
11. Princess of Wales.
12. Prince of Wales.
13. Duke of Edinburgh.
14. Duchess of Edinburgh.
15. Duchess of Albany.
16. Earl Cairns.
17. Lord Northbrook.
18. Lord Shaftesbury.
19. Lord Sherbrooke.
20. Lord Derby.
21. Marquis of Salisbury.
22. Earl Granville.
23. Duke of Argyll.
24. Duke of Westminster.
25. Lord Tennyson.
26. Lady Dudley.
27. Baroness Burdett-Coutts.
28. Lady Borthwick.
29. Duchess of Westminster.
30. Miss Rhoda Broughton.
31. Mr. Millais, R.A.
32. Sir Frederick Leighton, P.R.A.
33. Professor Ruskin.
34. Mr. Henry Herman (joint author of "Silver King," "Claudian," &c.).
35. Mr. Henry A. Jones (joint author of "Silver King," &c.).
36. Mr. J. Wilton Jones.
37. Mr. Alma Tadema, R.A.
38. Mr. Briton Riviere, R.A.
39. Mr. George Du Maurier.
40. Mr. G. A. Sala.
41. Mr. Joseph Derrick (author of "Confusion").
42. Mr. Richard Belt.
43. Mr. Edmund Yates (editor of the "World").
44. The Archbishop of Canterbury.
45. Cardinal Manning.
46. The Pope.
47. The Bishop of Ripon.
48. Mr. F. C. Burnand (editor of "Punch").
49. Mr. H. Labouchere, M.P. (editor of "Truth").
50. Mr. Arthur Goddard (editor of "Society").
51. Archdeacon Farrar.
52. Mr. C. H. Spurgeon.
53. Bishop of Manchester.
54. Dr. Hornby, Provost of Eton.
55. Rev. Edmond Warre, Head Master of Eton.
56. The Dean of Westminster.
57. Dr. Joseph Parker.
58. Lieut.-Col. Jay, H.A.C.
59. The Claimant.
60. Mr. G. R. Sims (author of "The Lights of London," &c.).
61. Mr. A. W. Pinero.
62. Mr. George Macdonald.
63. Mr. F. J. Fargus ("Hugh Conway").
64. Mr. H. J. Hitchins.
65. Mr. E. Russell.
66. Capt. Bashford.
67. "General" Booth.
68. Professor Tyndall.
69. Bishop of Peterborough.
70. Sir R. Cross, M.P.
71. Mr. Robert N. Fowler, M.P.
72. Mr. W. H. Smith, M.P.
73. Mr. H. Fawcett, M.P.
74. Sir Charles Dilke, M.P.

75. Sir James Paget.
76. Professor Huxley.
77. Sir William Gull.
78. Mr. Herbert Gladstone, M.P.
79. Mr W. E. Gladstone, M.P.
80. Mr. George Loveday.
81. Mr. W. E. Forster, M.P.
82. Mr. C. S. Parnell, M.P.
83. Mr. S. C. Allsopp, M.P.
84. Sir Wilfrid Lawson, M.P.
85. Sir M. A. Bass, M.P.
86. Sir Stafford Northcote, M.P.
87. Lord Randolph Churchill, M.P.
88. Mr Charles Bradlaugh.
89. Marquis of Hartington.
90. Sir William Vernon Harcourt, M.P.
91. Mr. J. G. Biggar, M.P.
92. Mr. J. Chamberlain, M.P.
93. Mr. John Bright, M.P.
94. Mr. Walter Joyce.
95. Mr. George Moore (Moore and Burgess).
96. Mr. Montagu Williams.
97. The Master of the Rolls (Sir W. Baliol Brett).
98. Lord Chief Justice Coleridge.
99. The Lord Chancellor (Lord Selborne).
100. Mr. Justice Hawkins.
101. Baron Huddleston.
102. Mrs. Weldon.
103. General Sir Archibald Alison.
104. General Sir W. Owen Lanyon.
105. Lord Alcester.
106. General Sir Evelyn Wood.
107. Field-Marshal the Duke of Cambridge.
108. General Lord Wolseley.
109. Major-General Drury-Lowe.
110. General Sir F. Roberts.
111. Colonel Burnaby.
112. Mr. W. Whiteley.
113. Sir Julius Benedict.
114. Baker Pasha.
115. General Gordon.
116. Mr. John Brinsmead.
117. Mr. George Fordham.
118. Mr. Fred. Archer.
119. Mr. Eugene C. Stafford.
120. Sir Arthur Sullivan.
121. Mr. W. S. Gilbert.
122. Mr. R. D'Albertson.
123. Mr. C. Alias.
124. Mr. W. Holland.
125. Mr. Arthur Roberts.

126. Miss Minnie Palmer.
127. Miss Fannie Leslie.
128. Mr. Fred. Leslie.
129. Miss Marie Linden.
130. Mr. J. L. Toole.
131. Mr. E. Royce.
132. Miss Nellie Farren.
133. Mr. Edward Terry.
134. Miss Violet Cameron.
135. Miss Florence St. John.
136. M. Marius.
137. Miss Kate Vaughan.
138. Mr. George Grossmith.
139. Mr. Wilson Barrett.
140. Miss Eastlake.
141. Mr. Sims Reeves.
142. Mr. William Farren.
143. Mr. Henry Neville.
144. Mr. Henry Irving.
145. Miss Ellen Terry.
146. Mr. Augustus Harris.
147. Miss Lingard.
148. Madame Sara Bernhardt.
149. Mr. Charles Warner.
150. Mr. Bancroft.
151. Mrs. Bancroft.
152. Mr. Forbes Robertson.
153. Mrs. Kendal.
154. Mr. W. H. Kendal.
155. Mr. Kyrle Bellew.
156. Mrs. Bernard-Beere.
157. Signor Salvini.
158. Miss Mary Anderson.
159. Mr. Harry Paulton.
160. Mr. Henry James.
161. Mr. W. S. Penley.
162. Mr. Harry Jackson.
163. Mr. H. Beerbohm Tree.
164. Mr. Edgar Bruce.
165. Mr. Charles Collette.
166. Mr. George Barrett.
167. Mrs. Stirling.
168. Mr. Cecil Brookfield.
169. Mr. Frederick Thorne.
170. Mr. Thomas Thorne.
171. Mr. Howard Paul.
172. Mrs. Langtry.
173. Mr. George Keogh.
174. Mr. W. J. Hill.
175. Mr. Lionel Brough.
176. Miss Fortescue.
177. Mr. Edward Righton.
178. Mr. Philip E.ck.

merely its theatrical standing but its growing status as a national institution, at which leading figures were welcomed not only to a performance but also to the social occasions Irving delighted to host in the restored 'Beefsteak Room', and occasionally on the stage itself. Henry Arthur Jones, his pen perhaps sharpened by Irving's rejection of *Michael and His Lost Angel,* commented: 'He would spend a thousand pounds to entertain Colonial Premiers. He would probably have grudged a thousand pounds to an English author as an extravagance.'[59] The basis of the Lyceum programme, with new productions interspersed with revivals of old favourites and even failures — *King Lear*, for example, was staged once a week during the early run of *Becket* — precluded the 'milking' of popular successes. Had Irving relied on the Lyceum's takings alone, his accounts would have run into the red far sooner. He had, however, two additional sources of income: provincial and American tours. He came to the Lyceum just as the golden age of provincial touring dawned, and during his years there an autumn tour was a regular feature of his programme, leaving its mark in the shape of the various Lyceum Theatres built in his honour, and supplementing his takings handsomely.

His American tours were even more profitable, and marked a new departure in every sense. While English actors had toured the New World throughout the century, a complete company playing an extensive 'classical' repertory was only feasible under late nineteenth-century travel conditions. Charles Wyndham, who had pioneered the idea of company touring in America, preceded Irving by twelve months on a coast-to-coast tour with his Criterion ensemble, offering a modest repertory of farces 'from the French'. In all Irving undertook eight American tours, usually of some six months' duration, and all save the last (1903 – 4) greatly aided by Ellen Terry as leading lady. Certain plays featured regularly — *The Bells, The Merchant of Venice, The Lyons Mail* — while the later tours offered at least one novelty: *Faust, Henry VIII, Becket, King Arthur.* As far as accounts survive (up to 1898 only), these American tours proved consistently rewarding, that for 1892 – 93 earning a profit of £24,330, over £10,000 more than the most successful season at the Lyceum itself.[60]

It is clear that Irving's acceptance of the American invitation in 1883 was a turning-point in his fortunes. His departure was made the occasion of two national tributes in a single week, a public dinner

# FAREWELL!!!
*Grand Tableau*—THE APOTHEOSIS OF IRVING.

*[Cheers, sobs, and Curtain falls to the tune of "Yankee Doodle."*

Gladstone (Prime Minister) and Earl Granville (Foreign Secretary) bid farewell to
Irving as he leaves on his first North American tour, 1883. Cartoon by 'J.G.'

for 500 (with 400 ladies including Ellen Terry looking on) at the St James's Hall, and a private dinner for 100 at the Garrick Club. These gestures raised Irving to the status of an Ambassador-Extraordinary and prompted the suggestion by Gladstone (conveyed through Lord Chief Justice Coleridge, who presided at the St James's Hall) of a knighthood. Irving's refusal was couched in interesting terms:

> He thinks that it would be very *ill* taken, instead of well, by his profession & like a gentleman & true artist as he is he wishes before all things to stand well with his profession and not seem to be put over them.[61]

He had, in fact, been licensee of the Lyceum for less than five years, and his suspicion that such an honour might be resented in the profession was not without grounds. Barry Sullivan declined an invitation to the Garrick Club Dinner, telling Bancroft, who presided, that 'he could not bring himself to acknowledge the justice of that position to which Irving had undoubtedly attained'.[62]

The old actor died in 1891 and thus was spared the mortification of witnessing Irving's knighthood four years later. By this time not only had Irving confirmed his pre-eminence — in America as well as at home. He had inspired a number of his contemporaries, including Bancroft, Wyndham, and Hare, and juniors, some like Alexander apprenticed to the Lyceum, to extend by their endeavours the prestige he conferred on the theatre. He was now not only *primus,* but *primus inter pares*, and the knighthood which might have caused offence when offered by Gladstone in 1883 was the subject of universal congratulation when recommended by Rosebery in 1895. The stage's new status even survived the setback in the same week as Irving's knighthood was announced of the downfall of London's most successful playwright, Oscar Wilde.

In a famous essay Max Beerbohm claimed to have caught sight of Irving in a brougham en route for the train to Windsor and the accolade:

> His hat was tilted at more than its usual angle, and his long cigar seemed longer than ever; and on his face was a look of such ruminant, sly fun as I have never seen equalled. I had but a moment's glimpse of him; but that was enough to show me the

soul of a comedian revelling in the part he was about to play —
of a comedic philosopher revelling in a foolish world. I was sure
that when he alighted on the platform of Paddington his bearing
would be more than ever grave and stately, with even the usual
touch of Bohemianism obliterated now in honour of the honour
that was about to befall him.[63]

If such was Irving's expression, it could be evidence that he realised
his knighthood was not only the summit of his achievement but the
start of his decline. The problem of finding plays for a leading man
approaching sixty and a leading lady nearly fifty mounted. For
Queen Victoria's Diamond Jubilee celebrations, during which she
extended Royal recognition of the stage by knighting Bancroft, the
Lyceum could only offer *Madame Sans-Gêne*, with Ellen Terry as a
comic laundress supported by Irving as a comic Napoleon. The rest
of his career comprised a mixture of good intentions, poor health,
and bad luck. The destruction of his scenic stores under the railway
arches at Southwark in February 1898 prompted his agreement to
the formation of the Lyceum Theatre Company, in order to spare
him financial responsibility and save his flagging strength for acting.
The effect was quite opposite to the intention. A disciple, H. A.
Saintsbury, points out that these setbacks 'did not affect his art, may
be gave it a finer edge, added poignancy to the martyrdom of Becket,
the misery of Mathias, the isolation of Shylock. But the manager was
broken'.[64] Hence perhaps arose his untimely choice of *Coriolanus*
and increasingly desperate reliance on second-rate Sardou, involving
reckless expenditure on *Robespierre* and later *Dante*.

After leaving the Lyceum and parting with Ellen Terry in 1902,
Irving's course led him increasingly to touring, both in the provinces
and America, interrupted by illness and two brief seasons at Drury
Lane. It is customary to deplore the financial necessity which drove
him to death in harness, and to point out that his modest estate,
£20,527, derived entirely from the sale of his treasured library. But
Henry Arthur Jones insisted that 'he had a lucky, noble death',[65] and
the extraordinary respect shown both him and his profession by a
funeral in Westminster Abbey and obituary tributes would hardly
have been paid if, like Macready, he had survived in retirement for
twenty years.

It is also customary to contrast Irving's declining fortunes with the
success during the last years of his life of competitors such as

*SIR HENRY IRVING, TO SIR S. BANCROFT:*—" DELIGHTED THAT WE ARE ON

IN THE SAME SCENE AGAIN, OLD FRIEND !"

Irving, knighted in 1895, is seen welcoming Squire Bancroft,
knighted in 1897. Cartoon by 'A.B.' (Alfred Bryan).

Wyndham, Alexander, and Tree. In the final analysis, however, Irving's greatest achievement was to make their success possible. The acceptance of the Lyceum as a temple of art prepared the public for other endeavours, many of which ran counter to Irving's own aims. Alexander encouraged Wilde and Pinero, Wyndham developed Jones's craft, and between them these writers brought about the renaissance of English drama which Irving neglected. Even the revolt against this Society drama which Shaw and Granville-Barker voiced at the Court, was only possible because during the preceding quarter-century the English theatre under Irving's leadership had recovered its self-respect, and with it the means of self-criticism. The playgoer who preferred Sloane Square to the Strand may have turned his back on the actor-managers, but without their efforts there would have been no 'thinking man's theatre', and Shaw and Galsworthy would probably have remained novelists, like Dickens and Thackeray before them. Irving himself belonged to the Victorian era, but he led the theatre into the twentieth century and those who followed took their rewards.

NOTES

1  Christopher St John (Editor), *Ellen Terry and Bernard Shaw: A Correspondence* (1949), p. xxiv.
2  Edith Craig and Christopher St John (Editors), *Ellen Terry's Memoirs* (1933), p. 210.
3  E. Gordon Craig, *Henry Irving* (1930), p. 62. See also David Mayer (Editor), *Henry Irving and 'The Bells'* (1980).
4  *Memoirs*, p. 82.
5  Laurence Irving, *Henry Irving: The Actor and His World* (1951), p. 457.
6  *Memoirs*, p. 82.
7  Laurence Irving, p. 305.
8  Ibid., p. 240.
9  H. A. Saintsbury and Cecil Palmer (Editors), *We Saw Him Act* (1939), p. 99.
10  *Memoirs*, p. 232.
11  *Pall Mall Gazette*, 31 December 1888, p. 4.
12  *Memoirs*, p. 161.
13  Ibid.
14  *Punch*, 14 May 1881, p. 225.
15  M. Willson Disher, *The Last Romantic* (1948), p. 91.
16  Henry James's views are most readily available in *The Scenic Art* ed. Allan Wade (1949). For the early performances see pp. 109-10; for *The Lady of Lyons*, p. 122; *The Merchant of Venice*, p. 143; *Romeo and Juliet*, p. 164; *Faust*, p. 221; *Cymbeline*, p. 283.

17  Ellen Terry, *Four Lectures on Shakespeare* (1932), p. 80.

18  Henry Arthur Jones, *The Shadow of Henry Irving* (1931), pp. 48-49.

19  *Memoirs,* p. 165.

20  Laurence Irving, p. 543.

21  Ibid., p. 544.

22  Bram Stoker, *Personal Reminiscences of Henry Irving* (1907), p. 144.

23  Information supplied by Professor Michael Booth.

24  Interviews with Irving in *Pall Mall Gazette* (13 September 1886) and with H. J. Loveday in *New York Tribune* (19 November 1887).

25  Unidentified interview with Irving in Percy Fitzgerald Collection, Vol. X, p. 127, Garrick Club.

26  *We Saw Him Act,* p. 307.

27  *Personal Reminiscences,* p. 156.

28  George Rowell, *Queen Victoria Goes to the Theatre* (1978), p. 106.

29  Joseph W. Donohue Jr. (Editor), *The Theatrical Manager in England and America* (1971), p. 209.

30  *We Saw Him Act,* pp. 322-23.

31  *Henry Irving,* p. 101.

32  *Memoirs,* pp. 123-34.

33  Ibid., p. 121.

34  E. Gordon Craig, *Index to the Story of My Days* (1957), p. 67.

35  *Personal Reminiscences,* pp. 116-17.

36  Ibid., pp. 159-60.

37  Ibid., pp. 69-70.

38  *Memoirs,* p. 189.

39  *The Times,* 30 August 1859. Reprinted in J. M. D. Hardwick, *Emigrant in Motley* (1954), p. 32.

40  *Memoirs,* p. 130.

41  Laurence Irving, p. 542.

42  Preface to *Hamlet* 'as arranged for the stage by Henry Irving' (1878), p. v.

43  *Pall Mall Gazette,* 13 September 1886.

44  *Memoirs,* p. 162.

45  Cited by Robert Speaight, *Shakespeare on the Stage* (1973), p. 66.

46  Laurence Irving, p. 402.

47  Information supplied by Professor Michael Booth.

48  *The World Behind the Scenes* (1881), p. 52.

49  *Memoirs,* p. 134.

50  Simon Nowell-Smith (Editor), *Edwardian England 1901 – 1914* (1964), p. 376.

51  Alan Hughes, 'Henry Irving's Artistic Use of Stage Lighting' in *Theatre Notebook* XXXIII:3 (1979), p. 103.

52  *Shakespeare on the Stage,* p. 57.

53  *Personal Reminiscences,* pp. 94-95.

54  Laurence Irving, p. 363.

55  *We Saw Him Act,* pp. 136-37.

56  Laurence Irving, p. 502.

57  Alan Hughes, 'The Lyceum Staff: A Victorian Theatrical Organization' in *Theatre Notebook* **XXVIII**:1 (1974), pp. 15-16.

58  Alan Hughes, 'Henry Irving's Finances: The Lyceum Accounts 1878—1899' in *Nineteenth Century Theatre Research* **I**:2 (1973), p. 82.

59  *The Shadow of Henry Irving,* p. 110.

60  Alan Hughes, 'Henry Irving's Finances', p. 85.

61  Laurence Irving, p. 410.

62  Ibid., p. 408.

63  Max Beerbohm, *Around Theatres* (1953), p. 400.

64  *We Saw Him Act,* p. 405.

65  *The Shadow of Henry Irving,* p. 72.

# CHAPTER THREE

# Gilding the Pictureframe

While the Lyceum under Irving occupied a unique position in the London theatrical world of the 1870s and 1880s, the most influential theatre during the 1870s was the little Prince of Wales's, tucked away in Tottenham Street, with a seating capacity of under 600.[1] Here Squire and Marie Bancroft set the prevailing tone, and though their house had a long if far from distinguished pre-history, most new theatres built in the wave of theatre construction which marked the period followed their pattern and scale. Thus miniature theatre became at once a standard and an ideal, and newly opened establishments like the Vaudeville, the Criterion, and the Court (this last significantly sited in a fashionable residential quarter) offered precise, polished performances in the Bancroft image.

Above all these new managements wooed successfully the audience which patronised the once seedy, now smart, Prince of Wales's. In one of his earliest recorded views of the English theatre, published in the *Galaxy* in 1877, Henry James gives a wry account of the entrée to this world:

> The first step in the rather arduous enterprise of going to the theatre in London is, I think, another reminder that the arts of the stage are not really in the temperament and the manners of

the people. The first step is to go to an agency in an expensive street out of Picadilly, and there purchase a stall for the sum of eleven shillings. You receive your ticket from the hands of a smooth, sleek, bottle-nosed clerk, who seems for all the world as if he had stepped straight out of a volume of Dickens or of Thackeray. There is almost always an old lady taking seats for the play, with a heavy carriage in waiting at the door; the number of old ladies whom one has to squeeze past in the stalls is in fact very striking. 'Is it good?' asks the old lady of the gentleman I have described, with a very sweet voice and a perfectly expressionless face. (She means the play, not the seat.) 'It is thought very good, my lady,' says the clerk, as if he were uttering a response in church . . .[2]

He concludes that the audience of which my lady is a member 'is well dressed, tranquil, motionless; it suggests domestic virtues and comfortable homes; it looks as if it had come to the play in its own carriage, after a dinner of beef and pudding', adding with Paris-educated hauteur: 'But you might spend your evening with them better almost anywhere than at the theatre'.[3]

It has been persuasively argued that the Bancrofts' achievement in drawing this audience had been forestalled by several managements in the 1850s,[4] and that with the Royal family's approval and lead, London playgoers were respectable and refined well before 1865 when Marie Wilton decided to lease the 'Dust Hole', as the theatre was then known, carpet the floors, and upholster the boxes in rosebud chintz. In the previous decade, however, managements were still bound by the routine of early Victorian theatregoing: long, oddly mixed bills, a swiftly changing repertoire, the need to provide 'something for everyone'. The Olympic, for example, fashionable as it became, had to offer burlesque and extravaganza at seasonable times, and could rarely venture on a full-length comedy or drama. The Bancrofts were fortunate in their timing: theatre audiences were not only more respectable but drawn from further afield, thanks to rapidly expanding railways. Thus the Prince of Wales's bill could concentrate increasingly on a single offering, and could be played unchanged for months, irrespective of the season. More particularly, the Bancrofts found almost from the start of their management a playwright perfectly suited to their needs.

For later generations Robertson and the Bancrofts are inseparable, and Robertson's plays the great, if not the only, achievement of their management. This was predictable, since the texts survive to be studied (unlike some of Irving's successes), and *Caste* at least keeps a modest hold on the stage, whereas the acting and production of the Bancrofts have to be taken on trust. To contemporaries, however, the attraction of the Prince of Wales's was much more than a Robertson play. The Bancrofts' management (including the transfer to the Haymarket) covered twenty years; Robertson survived for only six of these, and though his work was regularly revived, it was by no means seen as the milestone in English drama it now often appears. By the critics it was judged pleasing but slight. One of them, Percy Fitzgerald, in his *Principles of Comedy and Dramatic Effect* written at the height of Robertson's success (1870), dismissed *M.P.* like its predecessors as 'all agreeable, but it is not the drama — not comedy'.[5] This view of Robertson's work as mongrel-breed was accepted by the audience. In a much-quoted letter Dion Boucicault, whose finger was mostly and profitably on the public pulse, wrote to Mrs Bancroft after the failure at the Prince of Wales's of his 'modern comedy' *How She Loves Him* (1867):

> The public pretend they want pure comedy; this is not so. What they want is *domestic drama*, treated with broad comic characters. A sentimental, pathetic play, comically rendered, such as *Ours, Caste, The Colleen Bawn, Arrah-na-Pogue.*[6]

The association of *Caste* and *The Colleen Bawn* may seem incongruous but to their own audiences they were two examples of the same genre, one large and lavish, one small and intimate. As Boucicault put it:

> Robertson differs from me, not fundamentally, but scenically his action takes place in lodgings or drawing-rooms — mine has a more romantic scope.[7]

The 'comedy' in Robertson has grown more apparent with the years, as his 'domestic drama' takes on a quaint period flavour.

The triumph of the Bancrofts was therefore unchecked by his early death, aged forty-two, in 1871. The public continued to crowd into the Prince of Wales's and to support those theatres set up in its image, because the plays were undemanding and the performance marked by subtlety of playing and delicacy and detail in presentation.

In an age without film and only beginning to be touched by photography, this lifelike detail was an enormous attraction in itself. It had already conquered the melodrama with its command of movement, contrast, and spectacle. It now took over the interior scene and provided the sort of effect that only a tiny auditorium like the Prince of Wales's could achieve. In the Robertson years this was often associated with down-to-earth detail: the coat-pegs on the wall of the 'Owl's Roost' in *Society*; the falling leaves in *Ours*; the ham and cups-and-saucers in *Caste*. When in the 1870s the Bancrofts spread their net more widely, the effects were often more ambitious and elegant. In particular their essays in period revivals involved them in antiquarianism of the Charles Kean variety. For *The Merchant of Venice* (1875) E.W. Godwin's scholarly guidance was sought; for *The School for Scandal* (1874) the resources of the British Museum explored.

In retrospect the Bancrofts accepted that such methods were not always appropriate to their stage or style. Squire Bancroft decided that *The Merchant* failed because 'it looked so unlike a theatre, and so much more like old Italian pictures than anything that had been previously shown upon the stage',[8] and regretted choosing *The Rivals* (1884) because 'I am inclined to regard the old comedy as a bad selection for elaborate illustration'.[9] Moreover their 'elaborate illustration' was by no means confined to the scenery. Music, for example, became something of a mania in their period plays. A minuet in the second act of *The School for Scandal* was so prominently featured that it 'since has grown, through being followed in subsequent revivals, to be regarded as part of the play',[10] and was depicted on the drop-curtain when they moved to the Haymarket. Authenticity itself was not always rewarding; a frantic search for a real blackamoor to carry Lady Teazle's train eventually produced 'Biafra', an imp who misbehaved so outrageously on- and off-stage that he had to be replaced, and when another such was needed in *Masks and Faces* (1875), 'I contented myself with an imitation one', wrote Mrs Bancroft. 'The genuine article had been too much for me.'[11]

Delicacy was also the hallmark of acting at the Prince of Wales's, and a quality largely engendered by its early repertory. The influence of Robertson, both as playwright and 'stage-manager', with his repeated emphasis on underplaying and unstated emotion, developed into a recognised style, known as the 'school of reserved force'. This approach worked admirably for plays in the Robertson tradition (though regularly enhanced by the high spirits of Mrs Bancroft, once Marie Wilton, the burlesque actress), but was liable to falter if more widely applied. The failure of *The Merchant of Venice*, attributed by Bancroft to the over-authenticity of the stage-picture, might more readily be assigned to underpowered acting in at least one role. Charles Coghlan, an experienced and acclaimed performer in Robertson roles, reserved all his force for the dressing-room, changing his make-up as Shylock minutes before his first entrance. The result, according to his Portia, Ellen Terry, 'showed that night the fatal quality of *indecision*. A worse performance than his, carried through with decision and attack, might have succeeded, but Coghlan's Shylock was not even bad. It was *nothing*.'[12]

On the other hand, the production was a personal triumph for Ellen Terry, making her first appearance with the Bancrofts and trained, it may be noted, partly in the hurly-burly of the traditional Victorian theatre and partly by the taste and scholarship of such as G.F. Watts and Edward Godwin. Evidently she reserved her force for the last Casket scene:

> . . . I knew that I had 'got them' at the moment when I spoke the speech beginning, 'You see me, Lord Bassanio, where I stand.'
> 'What can this be?' I thought. '*Quite* this thing has never come to me before! *This is different*! It has never been quite the same before.'
> It was never to be quite the same again.[13]

The play came off after thirty-six performances. Soon she went on — to *Olivia* at the Court, and thence to the Lyceum.

The Bancrofts' repertory after Robertson's death underlines the limitations of both his and their methods. While several of their period revivals enjoyed substantial runs, and they could always put up a Robertson title when in difficulty, they found no recognisable successor. The new plays that won their public's favour, both at the Prince of Wales's and the Haymarket, were chiefly adaptations from Sardou, a reversal of Robertson's large measure of independence. *Diplomacy* (from *Dora*) with 326 performances in 1878—89 was easily the leader, with *Peril* (1876 — from *Nos Intimes*) also prominent at the Prince of Wales's, and *Odette* (1881) and *Fédora* (1883) at the Haymarket. Bancroft was conscious of this resort to borrowing, and defended himself by pointing out that it could have been worse. Writing of *Patrie* and Meilhac and Halévy's *Frou-Frou*, he blustered:

> In these plays we have always believed, and but for somewhat quixotic feelings at the date of their production, as to acting, as long as possible, only English plays, should have ventured on versions of one or both of them.[14]

The scarcity of Robertson's disciples was partly due to his early death and to the brief spell of six years in which all his theatrical success was packed. But certain other factors affected the short-lived attempts of the few followers he inspired. Of these James Albery with *Two Roses*, as has been suggested, most completely met the Robertsonian formula. Its characters are clearly modelled on his, headed by the scheming father of two attractive girls, one sensitive, one resilient, as in *Caste*, and the treatment emulates his delicate use of visual effects and unforced emotion. But try as he might (even exploiting the earlier play's title in *Two Thorns* and *Apple Blossoms*), Albery never repeated this feat — his one comparable success, to be examined later, being in the field of farce 'from the French' — and his later career was aimless and cut short.

The contrary is true of *New Men and Old Acres* (1868), since in it the veteran, Tom Taylor, paid tribute to a man twelve years his junior by writing on a wholly Robertsonian theme in a largely Robertsonian style. It was in fact submitted to the Prince of Wales's, but performed at the Haymarket (with Madge Robertson, the playwright's youngest sister), and later at the Court, when Shaw first saw and admired Ellen Terry. This story of the take-over of Cleeve Abbey (and ultimately its heiress, Lilian Vavasour) by good-hearted Samuel Brown, a merchant-prince from Liverpool, blends material from *Society* and *Caste*, the first and the best of the Robertson comedies for the Bancrofts. But it marked the end of Taylor's career as a comic dramatist.

The most significant of Robertson's few pupils was unquestionably W.S. Gilbert. He was also the frankest, acknowledging 'I have been at many of his rehearsals and learnt a great deal from them',[15] and though this tribute is more to Robertson, the 'stage manager', than to

Robertson the playwright, Gilbert also recognised a writing debt in several early pieces. Of these, *Sweethearts* (1874) was the most explicit and the most successful. The sycamore tree that grows from sapling to full height to denote the passing of thirty years (to the delight of the audience and the chagrin of the stage staff) is a wholly Robertsonian concept; so is the theme of the play, in which a capricious girl rejects her suitor and learns to regret it. Even the hastily contrived 'happy' ending is true to Robertson, though false to Gilbert.

*Sweethearts* was staged at the Prince of Wales's with Mrs Bancroft, and later her husband. Another Gilbert piece in this vein, *Charity* (1874), a curiously uneasy amalgam of borrowed sentiment and original humour, was performed at the Haymarket during the engagement there of Madge Robertson and her husband, W.H. Kendal. The association of these three with the Haymarket blends some of the most conventional and one of the most original elements of the London stage in the 1870s. The theatre itself represented all that was conservative: its managements were long — Webster stayed for fifteen years and Buckstone for twenty-five — and its companies and public loyal. It preserved oil lamps when every other West End theatre had gone over to gas, kept period comedy alive when melodrama swept across rival stages, and was the only patent theatre to be unaffected by the passing of the Theatre Regulation Act in 1843.

Yet in the 1870s, when still under the management of Buckstone, actor and author of many mid-Victorian 'comediettas', it brought forward the only cohesive series of truly English comedies of the post-Robertsonian era. Gilbert's major plays for the Haymarket (often called 'fairy comedies', though the term strictly applies only to *The Wicked World*) convey a single and consistent argument: that in an 'advanced' society its members say one thing and mean another, their ends being entirely selfish. This conclusion the author cloaked (as much for his own comfort as his audience's) in exotic or mythical dress — the Arabian Nights setting of *The Palace of Truth* (1870); the classical clothes of *Pygmalion and Galatea* (1871); as well as the fairyland of *The Wicked World* (1873) — and relieved with characteristically sly humour. Nevertheless his tone is often deeply cynical, and sometimes touches tragedy: the Queen of Fairyland in

Scene from Act II of *The Wicked World* by W.S. Gilbert (Haymarket, 1873), showing W.H. Kendal as Sir Ethais, and Madge Robertson (Mrs Kendal) as Queen Selene, with Marie Litton as Zayda (left) and Amy Roselle as Darine (right). Sketch by D.H. Friston.

*The Wicked World,* having lost her heart to a human (and with it her self-respect), upbraids the invaders:

> Are ye not content?
> Behold! I am a devil, like yourselves!

and Galatea turns back to stone to redress the injury she has innocently wrought on her creator. Add to these demands the extraordinary complexity of motivation in *The Palace of Truth* (its magic power offset by a 'talisman' which foreshadows the notorious 'lozenge'), and the intelligence of the late-Victorian audience, usually equated with a taste for puns and tear-jerking pathos, calls for some reassessment.

These three plays are in blank verse, a medium reserved by most Victorian dramatists for historical tragedy, but it may be questioned whether they gain by the choice. Gilbert's talent as a versifier lay in the brief lyric, as his *Bab Ballads* demonstrated. The measured line of his 'fairy' plays does nothing to lift the emotional scenes towards poetry, and positively hampers the comedy by stretching the jokes to fit the metre. The texts therefore inspire admiration for Madge Robertson and W.H. Kendal, who played the romantic leads in all three, and stirred their audiences to tears as well as laughter. In Gilbert's cause it should also be added that *Pygmalion and Galatea* proved a triumph for other players, notably the American Mary Anderson in her London appearances. It is in fact virtually the only verse play between those of Bulwer-Lytton and Tennyson to sustain its initial success.

After the Kendals had left the Haymarket, Gilbert wrote one more comedy for the company, *Engaged* (1877). Their absence seems to have influenced him and the play substantially. It is in prose, and the humour gains greatly from this emancipation, as Oscar Wilde was to demonstrate when borrowing several incidents from this play for *The Importance of Being Earnest*. It claims to be set in contemporary England (or Scotland — the plot runs through the border-line); its characters do not conceal their motives, but spell them out as if in the Palace of Truth itself. The hero is liberal with his affections and miserly with his money; the heroine professes life-long devotion and plans instant separation, because 'business is business'; the Scotsman who loves his sweetheart 'a'most as weel as I love mysel'', readily hands her over for 'twa pound' (having pushed up the price from 30/—). The tone remains as cynical and the point of view as jaundiced as in the plays which preceded it. Gilbert fell back on the description 'farcical comedy' to cover the absence of 'make-believe', and the public either welcomed it as outrageous farce or condemned it as heartless comedy.

A month later *The Sorcerer* opened at the Opera Comique, setting its author on an operatic course which henceforward only occasionally turned back to the 'legitimate' drama. Clearly the material and artistic success of the Savoy Operas largely settled Gilbert's career, but his four major Haymarket comedies suggest their author was looking for just such a resolution of his dilemma. The frequency with which he diluted his cynicism with sentiment (aspiring to poetry and even tragedy) or facetious humour indicates a reluctance to accept his own valuation of human nature. The absence of such compromises from *Engaged* had perhaps opened his own eyes as well as the public's. The attraction of blending his comic irony with pleasing melody, apparent from his earliest efforts, had won him artistic approval in the German Reeds' programmes at the Gallery of Illustration, and popular success with *Trial by Jury*. It is regularly asserted that Gilbert cherished his plays above his librettos. Apart from the certainty that he would never despise what had made him rich and famous, one may also conclude from the evidence of his Haymarket series that he was content to turn from the wicked world of the 'legitimate' drama to the musical charms of *The Sorcerer* and the operas which followed.

Gilbert's withdrawal from the Haymarket coincided with the retirement of its actor-manager, Buckstone. Two years later the Bancrofts decided to transfer their activities from the Prince of Wales's. Squire Bancroft makes it clear that when offered other leases, they replied: 'No, the Haymarket only will tempt us',[16] a tribute to the shrine of old English comedy from an apostle of the new. Their opening night, on 31 January 1880, was memorable less for the performance on-stage (another revival of *Money*) than for the innovation which framed it — and for a noisy prologue performed in the house itself.

Among the alterations they carried out was the introduction of a simulated 'picture-frame', for which Bancroft (perhaps influenced by Wagner's example at Bayreuth) insisted on sinking the footlights and concealing the orchestra. He certainly emphasised the influence *his* example had on the Continent, citing opera houses at Frankfurt and Brussels.[17] The innovation was not universally popular, the correspondent of the *Graphic* claiming that 'it seems to reduce what is going on upon the stage to a mere picture overpowered by a heavy and elaborate setting'.[18] It did represent, however, the culmination of two movements, one gradual — the rejection of the Georgian apron-stage and proscenium-doors — the other recent: the Bancrofts themselves had set the pace in making visual exactness the hallmark of their productions, and it was appropriate that they should complete the process in this way.

The performance in the house consisted of a twenty-minute uproar from the cheaper seats, with the refrain: 'Where's the pit?' In moving to the heart of theatreland with its proportionally higher costs, the Bancrofts had decided to convert the whole of the Haymarket parterre to stalls, a decision partly forced on them by the house's retention of a Georgian system of upper tiers encircling the pit, without cantilevered balconies which could provide cheaper accommodation beneath them. The close parallel between this movement, whereby the stalls had been encroaching on the pit for some years, and that of the proscenium-arch consuming the apron-stage is apparent. The protest proved no more than a safety-valve; the stalls survived intact, and the pit receded at other theatres, unreserved seats being increasingly confined to the gallery.

In the event the Bancrofts' tenure of the Haymarket proved something of an anti-climax. Their repertoire changed little, though runs were shorter in the larger house. Virtually the only novelty was their production of *Lords and Commons* (1883), an early piece by Pinero, who had moved to the Haymarket from the Lyceum and appeared in their revival of *The Rivals*, though neither his Sir Anthony Absolute nor his comedy was a conspicuous success. It was predictable that Mrs Bancroft would find good parts scarcer as her burlesque days receded and her comic range contracted. Her husband noted that the season 1883—84, in which her appearances were fleeting, 'was the least successful we knew at the Haymarket Theatre' (though he insisted loyally that the takings would have given much satisfaction at the Prince of Wales's).[19] There was also strong competition not only from Irving at the Lyceum but from old friends like Hare and the Kendals at the St James's. In 1885, when he was forty-four and his wife forty-six, they decided to retire from management, and though both lived to be over eighty, their subsequent appearances were few, culminating in Bancroft's knighthood in the Diamond Jubilee honours.

The contrast with many Victorian actors who played virtually to the end of their lives is striking. The simple truth — itself a telling comment on the growing prosperity of the theatre — was that they had no need to act. The morning after their farewell performance at the Haymarket, a van drew up outside their Cavendish Square home to deliver the bouquets and other tributes showered on them the night before. Mrs Bancroft records the exchanges of a couple of passers-by:

'What's all this mean?' said one.
'It's either a weddin' or a funeral,' was the reply.
'Who lives here?'
'Oh! *I* know why: it's the Bancrofts' 'ouse; they've jist 'ad a heap of money left them by a relation wot insists on their leavin' the stage!'[20]

The comment was truer than its author realised. The 'relation' was material success.

John Hare and the Kendals readily assumed the roles they had resigned. Their links with the Bancrofts were close and significant. Hare had served a long apprenticeship at the Prince of Wales's, creating parts as diverse as Sam Gerridge in *Caste* and 'Beau' Farintosh in *School*. He was living proof of the replacement of the old 'line of business' by closely observed character-acting. Although Mrs Kendal was Robertson's sister, she had never in fact appeared with the Bancrofts in his plays, but she and her husband contributed greatly to the success of their productions of two Sardou adaptations, *Peril* and *Diplomacy*, in the mid-1870s. Their association with Hare was first formed at the Court in 1875, interrupted by their move to the Prince of Wales's, but resumed in 1879. Later that year they moved their scene of operations to the St James's, like the Prince of Wales's, a theatre with a long but decidedly chequered history, to which they rapidly attracted a regular and distinguished public, putting it firmly on the theatrical map.

Their repertoire, both at the Court and more particularly at the

St James's, marked a logical continuation of the Bancrofts' during their later years of management. There was the same dependence on translation from the French: an early appearance at the Court, for instance, was in *A Scrap of Paper* (1876), one of several versions of Sardou's *Les Pattes de Mouche* popular during these years, and their first offering at the St James's was a transfer of *The Queen's Shilling* (1879), taken from *Un Fils de Famille,* by Bayard and Biéville. These French imports seem to have aroused no xenophobia — *The Queen's Shilling* was welcomed as 'that pure English comedy'[21] — and both Hare and the Kendals increasingly loosened their links with the authors who had served their earlier careers. Hare, for example, after sponsoring two 'neo-Robertsonian' successes at the Court — *New Men and Old Acres* in revival and *Olivia* — turned chiefly to 'Society' plays. After moving from the Haymarket, the Kendals acted in one last Gilbert — *Broken Hearts* (1875), a bruising experience for all concerned — and then broke off communication with their former associate, a rift that was only healed on the day he died.

To a large extent the character of the St James's was established by its leading lady. Madge Robertson had endeared herself to the Haymarket audience as a young, beautiful, sometimes tragic figure: Galatea to a number of Pygmalions. Mrs Kendal was made of sterner stuff: handsome, capable, but scarcely vulnerable, although commanding pathos when required. Her high opinion of her husband's looks and ability was not always shared by others, but Hare was content to play character roles and guide the fortunes of the management. They attempted the occasional poetic drama — including Tennyson's *The Falcon* (1879) and *As You Like It* (1885) — and even a version of *Black-Ey'd Susan,* adapted by W.G. Wills as *William and Susan* (1880), but their winning streak continued to be 'strong' drama from the French.

Many of these were put together — as the Bancrofts' had been — by theatrical journeymen such as Sydney Grundy, a prolific, dependable, and quite unoriginal worker in this field, who manufactured *A Wife's Sacrifice* (1886) for them from *Martyre* by D'Ennery and Tarbe. By far the most interesting of the sources on whom they depended at the St James's, however, was the still emerging talent of A.W. Pinero, the interest arising as much from the limits they imposed as the opportunities they offered. Thus two of his assignments were conventional *théâtre utile*: *The Ironmaster*

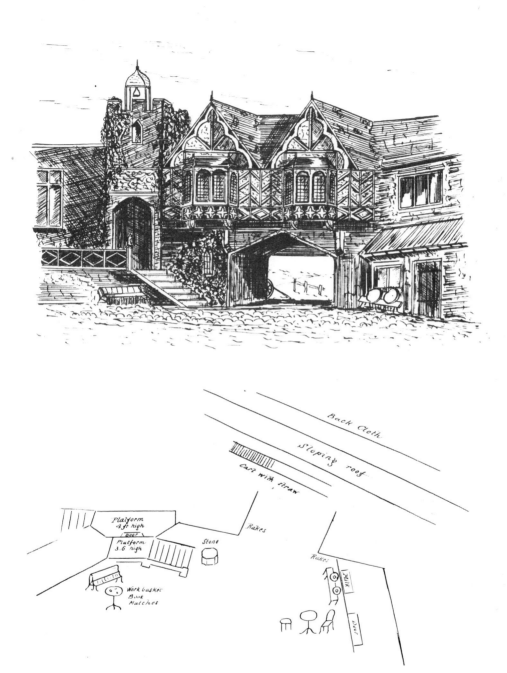

*The Squire* by A.W. Pinero (St James's, 1881). The elaborate setting for Act I (The Court, Prior's Mesne). Pen-and-ink drawing and corresponding ground-plan from an annotated MS copy, once in the possession of W.H. Kendal.

(1884), from Ohnet's *Le Maître des Forges,* with its central figure of a Captain of Industry marrying into Society but rejected by his wife, and *Mayfair* (1885, from *La Maison Neuve* by Sardou), a tale of wealth gained and happiness lost.

All these choices were tastefully staged, strikingly dressed, capably acted — pictures remarkable for detail, quite lacking in depth. But in between, the St James's also housed three of Pinero's early original plays, including *The Squire* (1881), which achieved some notoriety through the charges brought against it of plagiarising *Far from the Madding Crowd.* The resemblance of the central situation to the relationship of Bathsheba Everdene, Sergeant Troy, and Gabriel Oak, seems to have been unpremeditated, but it could not be denied that the St James's management had rejected J.W. Comyns Carr's dramatisation of Hardy's novel just before they accepted *The Squire.*[22] The production itself was noted for the completeness of the staging, which applied to its rural scenes the elaboration more usually lavished on drawing-room drama. Mrs Kendal quoted with approval a press comment that 'it wafted the scent of hay over the footlights',[23] thus adding another dimension to the pictorial theatre. The Harvest Chorus, however, struck an intriguing (and decidedly post-Bancroft) note of irony, coming as it did hard upon 'the Squire's' discovery that her secret marriage was bigamous and her child would be born illegitimate:

*At a signal from Gunnion a simple rustic chorus is sung to the accompaniment of Robjohn's fiddle.*

| A WOMAN: | What have you got for me, Goodman? |
|---|---|
| ALL THE WOMEN: | Say — a — a — a — ay! |
| MEN: | Laces and rings and womanly things |
| | Upon our harvest day — a — a — a — ay! |
| A WOMAN (*holding up a baby*): | |
| | What's for your baby boy, Goodman? |
| ALL THE WOMEN: | Say — a — a — a — ay! |
| MEN: | Baubles and milk and a robe o'silk |
| | Upon our harvest day — a — a — a — ay! |

Much more in keeping with the Hare-Kendal tradition was the preceding Pinero piece, *The Money-Spinner* (1880), which marked his graduation from curtain-raisers. With its French setting and several aristocratic characters (Lord Kengussie, 'Baron' Croodle) it reflected the *pièces bien faites* which Pinero was studying at the time, but the story attempted some subtlety of motivation, foreshadowing his later work. The heroine's nickname (recorded in the title) is earned by her skill at cards, which she desperately employs to rescue her feckless husband from ruin. In staging *The Money-Spinner*, Hare proved a true alumnus of the Robertson school, with cards replacing cups and saucers for its most telling moments. The prompt-copy was supplemented by a 'Card Scheme'[24] setting out the details of the four crucial hands played in the climactic scene:

No. 1   MILLICENT to deal   PINK
No. 2   KENGUSSIE to deal   BLUE
No. 3   MILLICENT to deal   BLUE
No. 4   KENGUSSIE to deal   PINK

with every card in each hand listed. It even recorded changes introduced during performances for Millicent's acquisition of the Ace of Spades in the crucial hand:

'In '85 Bus[iness] altered, MILLIE taking card from top of pack as KENGUSSIE turns his back, putting her own under candlestick.'

A later Pinero, *The Hobby Horse* (1886), mixed satire with sentiment instead of stretching out to farce, as the theme invites. Here an attractive woman married to an elderly and eccentric husband finds consolation under an alias in good works, only to win the heart of the unsuspecting curate of the East End parish she patronises. These misunderstandings, which might prove the life-blood of a farce, block the arteries of allegedly responsible characters. Throughout their career, however, the Kendals set their faces firmly against farce. Long before she achieved the distinction of a DBE in 1926, Mrs Kendal was proud to be dubbed 'The Matron of the Drama'. In 1884 she was invited to address the British National Association for the Promotion of Social Science at Birmingham (an honour which preceded by more than a decade Irving's knighthood) and chose to devote a substantial part of her address to an attack on farce:

At the present time . . . audiences enjoy a whole evening of farce, and farce of a very remarkable nature. What, in reality, can be a

more painful spectacle than that of an innocent and unsuspecting
wife, being hoodwinked and deceived by a graceless and profligate
husband? Years ago it would have formed the groundwork of a very
pathetic play, if not of a tragedy; but now it is a never-failing source
of delight to the lover of elongated farce; and the greater the
innocence of the wife, and the more outrageous the misconduct of
the husband, the louder are the shrieks of laughter with which their
misunderstandings are received.[25]

Though no one could call Pinero's farces 'a painful spectacle', these
views explain his switch of interest from the St James's to the Court,
where his first sustained successes were won.

The Hare-Kendal management quitted the St James's in 1888.
Hare had accepted an invitation to direct the newly-built Garrick,
opening with Pinero's *The Profligate*, and going on to stage *The
Notorious Mrs Ebbsmith* and — elsewhere — *The Gay Lord Quex*, all
milestones in a later chapter. The Kendals had agreed to tour
America, and this break in their careers proved a serious obstacle to
their recovery of a leading place on the London stage. Their
association with Hare at the St James's had raised that theatre to an
eminence it had never consistently achieved before, but it was
George Alexander, taking over in 1891, who was to reap the harvest.
Ironically Mrs Kendal spent a good deal of her later career touring in
a play by Pinero, originally produced — at the St James's — by
Alexander: *The Second Mrs Tanqueray*.

The 'farce of a very remarkable nature' at which Mrs Kendal
pointed an accusing finger to her Birmingham audience of social
scientists was undoubtedly linked in her mind with the Criterion
rather than the Court. The two theatres make an interestingly
contrasted study: both built in the early 1870s (though the Court was
rebuilt on an adjoining site in 1887), both closely associated with
farce. Here, however, the resemblance ends; the Court, as has been
seen, enjoyed success under changing managements. The Criterion,
after a brief and undistinguished opening, came under the direction
of Charles Wyndham, and remained so for the rest of his life. This
energetic comedian had served as a surgeon in the American Civil
War, and was later responsible for touring a chiefly Robertsonian
repertoire in the Middle West. Before moving into the Criterion,
however, he had established himself as a farçeur with *Brighton*
(1874), an adaptation of Bronson Howard's American farce, *Saratoga*,

and it was *Brighton* with its breathless series of amatory escapades that set the tone for Wyndham's management.[26]

The design of the theatre, opened earlier that year, was original and significant. It formed part of a larger complex, sited in the heart of the West End at Piccadilly Circus, and comprising besides the Criterion itself (originally designated 'the Lesser Hall') a ballroom and several restaurants. The building in fact took over some of the functions of the early music-hall, since that form of entertainment was finding a growing public of its own, although the lay-out suggested that the sponsors of the Criterion enterprise looked to a smarter audience than the music-hall encompassed. With Wyndham's arrival, the theatre itself, planned entirely underground, also seemed to solicit those patrons who twenty years earlier would have favoured the 'Coal Hole' and Evans' Song-and-Supper Rooms, or other resorts of the well-to-do young. Writing in 1882 the sternly Scots William Archer dismissed Wyndham's taste: 'His house might be rechristened the Club-Smoking-Room Theatre, so far as the plays presented are concerned',[27] and while this picture of a 'Men Only' establishment lacks foundation, there is plenty of evidence to suggest that the Criterion did fulfil for pleasure-seeking London playgoers the function of the Palais Royal in Paris.

Most of the plays presented are forgotten, though their titles — *The Great Divorce Case, Hot Water, Fourteen Days* — suggest something of their style. Another, *On Bail* (1877), by a somewhat unexpected author in this context, W.S. Gilbert, is more informative than it appears, since *On Bail* was adapted from *Le Réveillon* by Meilhac and Halévy, and *Le Réveillon* was also the basis of Johann Strauss's *Die Fledermaus*. It tells the familiar tale of the husband who insists on going to 'gaol' by way of a masked ball where he meets in disguise the wife he left weeping at home, and accurately defines the scope of a Criterion farce. To the more inhibited playgoers of the 1870s, a visit to the Criterion was the equivalent of Eisenstein's and Rosalinda's outing to the ball in *Die Fledermaus*, except that they took their pleasures vicariously. Their wives might accompany them; their neighbours might not, though they would certainly learn of the adventure, and envy them for it.

The origins of *On Bail* supply another clue to the Criterion's policy; its products were almost always 'from the French'. One of the few English farces staged by Wyndham during his regime was another Gilbert, *Foggerty's Fairy* (1881), which proved one of his few failures. Gilbert's style was too fantastic and taxing for the Criterion audience. However, Wyndham's aim of making the Criterion the Palais Royal of London involved major difficulties of translation, both geographic and textual. What was acceptable and appreciated by sophisticated Parisians was neither acceptable to the Lord Chamberlain's Examiner of Plays nor appreciated by the affluent class of playgoer Wyndham cultivated. His chief task as actor-manager was therefore to find both a play and an adaptor who could 'defuse' the potential bomb while leaving it ticking long enough to titillate his audience.

This 'defusing' process is best illustrated by his biggest success, *Pink Dominos,* which ran for 555 performances between 1877 and 1879. The original play in this case was *Les Dominos Roses* by Hénnéquin and Delacour, and the adaptor, James Albery, was by now glad to undertake this and other 'doctoring' for Wyndham. *Les Dominos Roses* offered an elaboration of the *Fledermaus* formula: two husbands pursue two masked ladies at a 'smart' restaurant, and inevitably the two ladies are their own wives, investigating their partners' apologies for absence from home. Albery's adaptation was suitably circumspect. The central scene was changed from a dubious establishment with *chambres separées* to Cremorne Gardens, Mecca of middle-class diversion. One subsidiary character, Fédora, an 'actress' from the Variétés, who is a strong counter-attraction in the original, becomes 'Miss Barron' who has 'promised Ma to be home by 1' (and keeps her word).

Even the dialogue underwent transmogrification. The two wives in the original discuss their husbands' shortcomings with an allusiveness reminiscent of Lady Fidget and her cronies in *The Country Wife*:

> MARGUERITE: Aujourd'hui l'éspèce 'mari' se dévise en deux
> catégories: les adroits et les maladroits, ceux qui ne font pas
> pincer et ceux — au contraire — qui —
> ANGELIQUE:  Ah! quelle horreur! (*Elle pose sa brodérie*)
> MARGUERITE: Il n'y en a pas d'autres — parmis les maris effectifs,
> bien entendu — parce que je ne te parle des invalides. Et encore
> parmi ceux là, il y en a tant de faux — qui reprennent du service
> dans l'armée irrégulière.

Such a passage would have set every alarm bell in St James's Palace ringing. The licensed copy of a later Criterion piece, *Truth* (1879), still bears the outraged comment: 'How is this word still here?'[28] (the offender being the 'transparent trousers' worn by a lady at a fancy dress ball). Albery therefore cut the Gaudian knot and rendered the passage cited from *Les Dominos Roses*:

> Show me the dog that won't take a bone. The only difference is the dog that is found out and the dog that isn't.

which earned *Pink Dominos* its licence, but might appropriately be termed 'neutering'.

If all Wyndham had to offer at the Criterion was French farce domesticated and house-trained, his regime would have proved brief. Like the Bancrofts and the Kendals, however, he offered his second-hand goods elegantly displayed and impeccably packaged. His own acting style, compact of speed and confidence, owed a good deal to Charles James Mathews and not a little to E.A. Sothern. It earned him the label of 'the electric light comedian' at a time when electricity was still a rare and sought-after commodity, in and out of the theatre. The Criterion studied its audience's comfort, offering power-assisted ventilation (doubtless a necessity in its underground location), coffee as well as stronger draughts, an illustrated programme instead of a playbill. It aimed to please; its electricity was carefully insulated against shock.

In the early 1880s, however, this motive power underwent a change of current. Wyndham himself had reached middle-age. His fame as a farceur had carried him across the Atlantic on a coast-to-coast tour with the Criterion Company which preceded by a year Irving's first transatlantic crossing. On his return he found a change taking place in the London theatre, consequent upon the Bancrofts' impending retirement. His response was a gradual conversion of the Criterion into a miniature Haymarket, specialising in the period comedies for which that theatre had always been known. Thus he revived in turn *Wild Oats, She Stoops to Conquer, London Assurance,* and *The School for Scandal.* But his biggest triumph of these years was appropriately in *David Garrick,* which he first revived in 1886, and could always rely on afterwards.

This was Robertson's earliest success, originally produced at the

Haymarket and looking backwards nostalgically to an authentic actor in a far from authentic situation — the star of Drury Lane called on to cure a young lady's infatuation by feigning drunkenness at the table, but losing his own heart and winning her hand in the process. *David Garrick,* both play and part, represented Wyndham's emancipation from French farce. Henry Arthur Jones, who was to write several later triumphs for him, analysed his magic in this one:

> He'd only two notes in his voice, but he could do anything with them.[29]

and after his death, the critic, W.L. Courtney, developed this idea:

> Nine men out of ten would tell you that Wyndham's voice was harsh and unmusical; nineteen women out of twenty would tell you that it was the most compelling and seductive thing in the world.[30]

His comment also showed how the Criterion had developed from the 'Club Smoking-Room Theatre' of Archer's scorn in 1882 to a matinee idol's throne by the end of that decade.

The parallel between Wyndham's period comedy at the Criterion and the Bancrofts' at the Haymarket is close, but a comparison between his series of farces and the contribution to that genre made at much the same time by the Court Theatre is more germane to the flowering of English drama. Here in the 1880s there assembled a team of farçeurs whose ensemble has been rivalled only by the company which held the stage of the Aldwych in the 1920s. Indeed the composition of the two teams was remarkably close: both included a pure and persecuted husband (Arthur Cecil; Robertson Hare), a knowing man of the world (John Clayton; Tom Walls), with his vacuous companion (Fred Kerr; Ralph Lynn), and not least a formidable matron (Mrs John Wood; Mary Brough). This striking resemblance between the dramatis personae of the Court farces in the 1880s and the Aldwych farces in the 1920s is perhaps stronger evidence of the abiding foundations of farce than the cyclic nature of theatrical history.

It also arose because both companies found a 'resident-dramatist' whose understanding showed off the skill of the resident-company. What Ben Travers understood in writing *A Cuckoo in the Nest,*

*Rookery Nook*, and their successors, Pinero had discovered when providing the Court with *The Magistrate* (1885), *The Schoolmistress* (1886), and *Dandy Dick* (1887). He had provided other companies with earlier farces, and he was to continue writing in this vein to the end, but the stimulus of the Sloane Square team drew an inspired response from him. Interestingly, *Dandy Dick* was the last production at the Court before it was rebuilt on a nearby site, and some of the magic was lost in the move. The new theatre was to stage two more Pinero farces (*The Cabinet Minister*, 1891, and *The Amazons*, 1893), with several survivors from the original company, but their appeal was limited, and Pinero did not find the true measure of the new Court until *Trelawny of the Wells* — a play about the transformation of an old theatre and the establishment of a new theatrical style — was staged there in 1898.

In his three 'major' farces Pinero put to splendid use the lessons in construction he had learnt from his apprenticeship to the French well-made-play under the Kendals. No line is superfluous; no link in the causal chain neglected. When in *The Magistrate* a waiter remarks that the balcony outside is 'not at all safe', it follows that the balcony will serve as the refuge for a succession of characters, and that the most innocuous will fall the furthest. When in *The Schoolmistress* the lady of the title informs her forgetful husband that 'our fire insurance expired yesterday — post the premium to the Eagle Office at once', it presages that Volumnia College will burn before the night is out. In this respect the farces show Pinero's skill more happily than the later 'problem plays' in which the elaborate structure sometimes seems a substitute for the character and content the form promises.

But if construction is their chief beauty, it is by no means the farces' only strength. There is a quality of innocence about the people that proclaims their freedom of French origin. The magistrate himself and the Dean of St Marvell's in *Dandy Dick* place their careers in grave jeopardy and learn their lessons from brutal chastisement through the most honourable of motives. Poskett's visit to the Hotel des Princes is truly in loco parentis; not for him the pursuit of pink dominos. The Dean's doping of the horse, Dandy Dick, is for the Cathedral Restoration Fund and the greater glory of God. Even Queckett's suspect gathering of 'two or three good fellows' in 'lodgings of humble bachelor' in *The Schoolmistress* serves to launch a newly-wed young couple on the voyage of life. Nothing could be further from a masked ball than a lark pudding and a quadrille.

Reference has been made to the promise of Pinero's earlier work when compared with that of an older practitioner like Sydney Grundy, but perhaps the clearest comparison at this stage is with H.J. Byron, a comrade of Robertson's and an enormously prolific playwright, who in 1875 achieved unprecedented success with a farce, *Our Boys*, which relied on the smugness of the Vaudeville audience to swallow such a joke as the 'Retired Butterman's' rebuke to his son for failing to see 'Vesoovius fizzin' ':

> That's wrong, you know. That's wrong. I didn't limit you, Charley. I said 'See everything', and I certainly expected as you'd insist upon an eruption.

The 1,362 performances of *Our Boys* and the 555 nights of *Pink Dominos* testify to the impressive growth of London audiences in the 1870s, and to the less impressive limits of their taste.

This was all too apparent to William Archer when he published *English Dramatists of Today* in 1882, in many respects an attempt to make bricks without straw (there are chapters devoted to such minor practitioners as F.W. Broughton and S. Theyre Smith), but an acknowledgement that houses could not be built without bricks. One complaint that Archer voiced loudly was the lack of published plays. Alone among the authors he considered W.S. Gilbert's work was widely available in a reading edition. For the rest he had to fall back on 'the quite unreadable form in which Mr French presents them to "the profession and amateurs" ',[31] and even that source was sadly deficient. 'I may mention that the expenditure of about a pound . . . procured for me every play on his list which could possibly be of the slightest use to me',[32] a comment passed not in praise of Mr French's prices but in criticism of his omissions.

These were chiefly a reflection of the still vexed state of theatrical copyright which, despite various measures over the previous fifty years, did not achieve full legal protection for the playwright until the acceptance of the Berne Convention in 1886, and the American copyright law of 1891. But the scarcity of both published plays and publishable playwrights with which Archer was confronted arose from wider causes. The twenty years following Robertson's death proved a period of great theatrical progress but mostly dramatic stagnation. The actor-managers' emphasis fell on presentation, not on what was presented, a feature as apparent in Irving's repertoire as in the Bancrofts' or Kendals'. Their policy paid off; audiences grew and were satisfied. Theatres continued to be built in impressive numbers: besides the Vaudeville, Court, and Criterion, on which some stress has been laid, the 1870s saw the opening of the Opera Comique and the Imperial. In the 1880s the Comedy, the Savoy, the Avenue, the Novelty, the new Prince of Wales's, Terry's, the Lyric, the Shaftesbury, and the Garrick were all built in central London alone. The rate of expansion speaks for itself.

New theatres bred new actor-managers, and steadily as the theatrical public increased, it also became more discriminating in the face of such a choice. Skill in acting and taste in staging could achieve much, but under intense competition another element was sought: originality in writing. It has been suggested that only one dramatist consistently offered this quality in the 1870s, and that by the end of that decade he had largely turned his attention to the musical stage. W.S. Gilbert's transfer of interest was timely. The comic opera supplied the audiences of the 1880s with something the legitimate drama lacked.

NOTES

1   See Richard Lorenzen, 'The Old Prince of Wales's Theatre: A View of the Physical Structure' in *Theatre Notebook* XXV: No. 4 (1971), p. 142.
2   Allan Wade (Editor), *The Scenic Art*, p. 100.
3   Ibid., p. 101.
4   Notably by Michael R. Booth in *The Revels History of English Drama* VI (1975), pp. 14-17.
5   Percy Fitzgerald, *Principles of Comedy and Dramatic Effect* (1870), 'Postscript', pp. 355-56.
6   Squire and Marie Bancroft, *Mr and Mrs Bancroft On and Off the Stage*, 7th edition (1889), p. 118.
7   Ibid.
8   Ibid., p. 212.
9   Ibid., p. 374.
10  Ibid., p. 188.
11  Ibid., p. 196.
12  *Ellen Terry's Memoirs*, p. 87.
13  Ibid., p. 86.

14 *Mr and Mrs Bancroft*, p. 150.
15 Interview with William Archer in *Real Conversations* (1904), p. 114, cited in numerous later studies.
16 *Mr and Mrs Bancroft*, p. 284.
17 Ibid., p. 294.
18 See R[ichard] S[outhern], 'The Picture-Frame Proscenium of 1880' in *Theatre Notebook* V: No. 3 (1951), pp. 59-61.
19 *Mr and Mrs Bancroft*, pp. 374-75.
20 Ibid., p. 410.
21 *Dame Madge Kendal. By Herself* (1933), p. 137.
22 See J.F. Stottlar, 'Hardy vs. Pinero: Two Stage Versions of *Far From the Madding Crowd*' in *Theatre Survey* 18: No. 2 (1977), pp. 23-43.
23 *Dame Madge Kendal*, p. 144.
24 Now in the Library of the Garrick Club.
25 *Dame Madge Kendal*, p. 193.
26 See J.W. Donohue (Editor), *The Theatrical Manager in England and America* (1971), pp. 189 et seq.
27 W. Archer, *English Dramatists of Today*, p. 76.
28 Now in the Lord Chamberlain's Collection of Playscripts deposited at the British Library (Manuscript Division).
29 Doris Arthur Jones, *Life and Letters of Henry Arthur Jones* (1930), pp. 209-10.
30 W.L. Courtney, *The Passing Hour* (1925), pp. 202-3.
31 *English Dramatists*, p. 6.
32 Ibid., p. 18.

# CHAPTER FOUR

# 'A New and Original Comic Opera'

In many respects music formed the backbone of the Victorian playbill. Not only was song and dance a prominent feature of the evening's entertainment, but the orchestra itself provided an essential dramatic element, especially as melodrama — by definition music and action — came to dominate the repertoire. In the early part of the period music regularly displaced speech at crucial points of the story, partly for legal reasons while the distinction between 'patent' and 'minor' theatres obtained, but essentially because for the early Victorian audience music carried greater emotional power and could generally exercise it, however large and unruly the house.

For the educated theatregoer music in the form of opera and ballet largely eclipsed the spoken drama. In the 1830s and 1840s Her Majesty's (as the Italian Opera House had been tactfully renamed) occupied a supreme position, and its summer seasons had a recognised place in the social calendar. After the abolition of the patents by the Theatre Regulation Act of 1843 the provision of opera multiplied. Covent Garden at once became an opera-house, in this capacity surviving the fire of 1856 and steadily overtaking Her Majesty's in prestige, while there were regular summer seasons of opera at Drury Lane into the 1870s, and occasional visits by French and German companies to the Lyceum and elsewhere.

In no department of Victorian drama was music more important than comedy. As the taste for full-length comedy gave way to that for the short farce usually offered as an afterpiece, so the main field of comic endeavour became the burlesque, extravaganza, and panto-mime, all three articulated by music. Although music was not an essential part of burlesque as earlier practised by Buckingham, Fielding, and Sheridan, the disappearance of the heroic drama on which they had concentrated their satire left a gap which Victorian practitioners were glad to fill with song, dance, and spectacle. Lacking the common ground of theatrical convention and language which had inspired *Tom Thumb* and *The Critic,* burlesque writers and audiences seized on broader targets: classical myth, Shakespeare, and melodrama. Often the authors had to signpost their objective by singling out a popular favourite, hence the 'travesty', and invite laughter by such recognised methods as commonplace thoughts from elevated characters and banal words to cherished melodies. The burlesque thus inherited from the ballad opera the tradition of music drawn from many diverse sources.

The pioneer of extravaganza, James Robinson Planché, regarded the term as 'distinguishing the whimsical treatment of a poetical subject from the broad caricature of a tragedy or serious opera, which was correctly termed a "Burlesque" '.[1] He was writing of his *Sleeping Beauty in the Wood* at Covent Garden in 1840, but he had already tackled fairy stories of this kind for the same manageress, Madame Vestris, at the Olympic, and his varied gifts as writer and designer equipped him to provide an entertainment subtle in humour and delicate in effect. Other writers lacked his flair; 'extravaganza' in the 1850s and 1860s became a term only loosely distinguished from burlesque by its freedom from 'travesty'. Often the terms were confused or even combined. At the same time pantomime grew even further away from its commedia dell' arte origins, already confined to the harlequinade in the second half, and began to encroach in its 'opening' on the fairy stories which provided Planché with the sources of extravaganza.

As long as all three forms figured prominently in the bills of most theatres, there was a common pool of performers on which managers drew: Madame Vestris played Shakespeare at Covent Garden, Frederick Robson, the uniquely talented interpreter of Shylock and Medea in burlesque versions, also led the Olympic Company in melodrama and farce. But with the increasing specialisation of theatres in the 1860s, certain houses made burlesque their principal offering. The Strand provided the springboard for Marie Wilton, a burlesque favourite in 'boy' parts, to graduate to Mrs Bancroft, directress of the Prince of Wales's. The Royalty, an obscure theatre hitherto, won success with burlesque in the 1860s and 1870s. More significantly, the Gaiety was opened by Hollingshead as a principally burlesque house in 1868, and established itself as the leading exponent of this style over the next two decades.

Another development of this period was the appearance of French operetta, particularly Offenbach's, in English versions. It is noteworthy that several of the early homes of this form also specialised in French farce, for example the Criterion and the Charing Cross, pointing to the identification in the public's mind of French operetta with risqué entertainment. It is unquestionable that the popular musical stage in the mid-Victorian period was regarded as suspect, both as to content and conduct. In 1866 the Parliamentary Select Committee into the theatre devoted much of its time to questioning the manager of the Alhambra (whose policy moved cannily between music-hall and operetta) about the coffee-room in which the ladies of the chorus were served.[2] Anti-theatrical prejudice, strongly entrenched over the years, held out longest and strongest against the ballet-girl and all she was believed to represent.

It was to allay such fears and cultivate those who held them that several 'musical' ventures sprang up in the 1860s. Prominent amongst such pioneers were Mr and Mrs German Reed, both of whom had turned their backs on a theatrical past (in Mrs Reed's case that of Macready's leading comédienne, Priscilla Horton) in order to offer an acceptable alternative to burlesque or operetta. In a succession of non-theatres, particularly the Gallery of Illustration (a deliberately cultural choice of name) in Regent Street, they assembled a company and programme which reassured and entertained an increasingly distinguished audience. That audience's taste and the company's talents provided an outlet for miniature extravaganza, closer to Planché (who wrote one of his last pieces, *King Christmas*, for them in 1871) than either burlesque or operetta, but offering wider scope for humour and, importantly, for specially composed music.

The opportunities offered by the German Reeds were taken by both Gilbert and Sullivan, though not together. Both Sullivan's

79

contributions were written with F.C. Burnand: *The Contrabandista* (1867) was part of an ambitious but costly season mounted at St George's Hall; *Cox and Box* (1869) was much closer to the Gallery of Illustration style. Adapted from John Maddison Morton's perennial farce, the latter had been written two years earlier for amateurs of no little distinction, the tenor being George Du Maurier. This 'triumviretta' conformed to the German Reeds' policy of small-cast works without chorus, and offered Sullivan scope for the adroit musical humour he was later to bring to the Savoy Operas.

Gilbert's part in the Gallery of Illustration programme was more substantial — five pieces over the period 1869 – 72 — and assumed a high degree of literary and theatrical expertise in their audience, as titles such as *A Sensation Novel* (1871), with each act called a 'volume', and *Happy Arcadia* (1872) suggest. Their interest as sources for the Savoy Operas has been recognised:[3] *Ages Ago* (1869), with the characters stepping out of picture-frames, clearly points to *Ruddigore*, and *Our Island Home* (1870), with castaways rescued by a pirate apprentice newly come of age, to *The Pirates of Penzance*. The intrinsic merit of these pieces, however, lies in their dexterous handling of complex identities and time-schemes, drawing on a vein of fantasy far subtler than their author dared attempt in the theatre itself. Gilbert's early work there fully illustrates the limitations and frustrations of writing for the musical stage. He was given an opening when Robertson recommended him to the St James's for its Christmas piece: *Dulcamara; or The Little Duck and the Great Quack* (1866), and during the next four years he wrote extensively for several burlesque companies, notably at the Royalty and Gaiety, where he contributed *Robert the Devil; or, The Nun, the Dun, and the Son of a Gun* (1868) to the opening programme. These apprentice pieces were inevitably cut to the prevailing pattern, with actresses as 'boys', puns in plenty, and the lyrics fitted to Nigger Minstrel melodies like the following from *Dulcamara*:

> If you say nay I can only say
> Skid-a-ma-link and a doodah day,
> Boodle, oodley, umshebay,
> And a hunky dorum, doodle day.

From such indignities he was rescued when Hollingshead at the

Gaiety, implementing a policy of commissioned scores, invited him to collaborate with Sullivan on *Thespis; or, The Gods Grown Old* (1871). (By an entirely characteristic twist this score was then lost.) *Thespis*, written for the resident company, with Nellie Farren in breeches and Toole in the title role, was pitched closer to burlesque than comic opera, being about theatricals and Greek gods, though not a travesty of a theatrical subject. By now Gilbert was beginning to establish himself as a 'legitimate' dramatist at the Haymarket and elsewhere, and *Thespis* marked the end of his work in the traditional form, though it took four years and a return to the Gallery of Illustration for *Happy Arcadia* before he was again paired with Sullivan — by a different impresario, D'Oyly Carte — on *Trial by Jury* (1875), announced as a 'dramatic cantata'. The description, very much in the German Reed vein, was a clear pointer to the future.

The theatre on which D'Oyly Carte settled when following up this success was the Opera Comique, a name which (despite the building's 'rickety' reputation) defined the entertainment he planned to offer. The billing of the Gilbert and Sullivan series placed much emphasis on their originality — 'original' features in the description of all but two of them — and seems picked to distinguish them from French imports, which would not only lack originality, but, more damaging, propriety. On the other hand, the various descriptive adjectives — 'nautical', 'melodramatic', 'aesthetic', 'supernatural' — relate closely to theatrical and literary sources, as do the alternative titles with their alliteration. The theatrical antecedents of *H.M.S. Pinafore* (1878) and *The Pirates of Penzance* (1880) are easily traced to nautical melodrama; those of *Ruddigore* (1887) to 'Gothic' drama. *The Sorcerer* evidently relates, like the earlier *Dulcamara*, to *L'Elisir d'Amore*, and *Princess Ida* (1884) was an acknowledged reworking of Gilbert's earlier burlesque, *The Princess*. *Iolanthe* (1882), announced quite simply as 'a Fairy Opera', seems thereby to disclaim 'originality' and own kinship with the 'fairy' plays. *The Mikado* (1885), *The Yeomen of the Guard* (1888), and *The Gondoliers* (1889) properly assert their independence; they are in every respect the most substantial of the series, but after the long break in the partnership there was a recognisable return to theatrical sources. *Utopia Limited* (1893) reflects Planché's interest in fantastic trappings for flesh-and-blood royalty, and *The Grand Duke* (1896) ends the collaboration where it had begun, with a theatrical troupe prominent amongst its characters. Throughout, the overlapping function of burlesque, extravaganza, and comic opera are illustrated.

The basis on which D'Oyly Carte set up his company owed much to the German Reeds, and sought successfully to attract their audience. The two leading comedians, George Grossmith and Rutland Barrington, were recruited from 'non-theatrical' quarters, and had to be nursed until fully-fledged. The consequences are apparent in the early operas, all less than full-length, with the comic performers underexposed and much of the comedy allotted to hero and heroine, a responsibility that tenors and sopranos are not invariably bred to sustain. Nevertheless the semi-permanent company proved a boon as the series progressed. Not only was the chorus used more extensively and enterprisingly; the principals were given increased scope for acting and singing. The growing confidence placed in Grossmith and the soubrette, Jessie Bond, is particularly striking. Major-General Stanley has one song and one passage of dialogue in the first act of *The Pirates of Penzance*. Cousin Hebe had neither solo nor dialogue in *H.M.S. Pinafore*, as originally written. Yet by *Ruddigore* Grossmith could be trusted with a 'dual' role (honest Robin and wicked Sir Ruthven) in the Lyceum tradition, while Jessie Bond encompassed the transformation of Mad Margaret into District Visitor. Their next appearances demanded even more of them: the pathos of Jack Point and the jealousy of Phoebe Meryll.

From the beginning of the series Gilbert set his mark firmly on the style and standards of performance. He had clashed frequently with earlier managers, and his quarrel with Hare and the Kendals over *Broken Hearts*, leading to a long estrangement, occurred just after the launching of *Trial by Jury*. With a financial as well as artistic interest in D'Oyly Carte's venture, he was determined to follow the example of his mentor, Robertson, and take charge of his own rehearsals. But Robertson's approach was evidently one of suggestion, not coercion. 'He had a gift' wrote his prize pupil, John Hare, 'peculiar to himself, of conveying by some rapid and almost electrical suggestion to the actor an insight into the character assigned to him.'[4] Gilbert's nature was more forceful, and the task of producing comic opera called for a stronger hand. Burlesque after Planché's lead had reverted to the hotch-potch of styles its subject-matter allowed. Robertson was dealing with actors; Gilbert was confronted by singers, and even more taxing, a chorus, by tradition lax in discipline if not in morals.

It was therefore a basic principle of Gilbert's work as a producer to impose uniformity on his chorus, and after an uncertain start in *The Sorcerer*, where the villagers of Ploverleigh seem to have strayed in from pantomime, the nautical drill of *H.M.S. Pinafore* provided exactly the discipline he demanded. The characteristic flavour of Savoy Opera owes much to the solidarity of its chorus, male and female, and to the strong contrast between their respective identities: rapturous maidens and dragoon guards; fairies and peers of the realm; Japanese gentlemen and schoolgirls. The loss of attack in *Utopia Limited* and *The Grand Duke* at the end of the series is attributable in part to their reversion to an 'assorted' chorus.

The discipline Gilbert imposed on his cast survives not only in more than a century of performances by the D'Oyly Carte Company, but in the prompt-books of productions and revivals he supervised. The hand of the tough taskmaster is recorded in an entry from that for *Iolanthe*:

> [Peers] take handkerchiefs out of coronets, wipe right eye, wipe left eye, rub their noses with handkerchiefs, and return them to coronets, which they replace on their heads.[5]

or during Nanki-Pooh's 'song of the sea':

> rowing action four times/twice *on* stage and twice *off*/hauling eight beats/then smack and hitch.[6]

There is a good deal of the sergeant-major's approach in such drill, so that it is refreshing to read the occasional practical hint:

> *Note.* — Peers being dressed in white silk tights, do not actually kneel, but only appear to do so. Peers allow their handkerchiefs to drop on stage as they lower their coronets, and then place coronets on handkerchiefs.[7]

Gilbert's authority in rehearsal derived not only from his status as librettist. He was also an accomplished draughtsman, as his illustrations for the *Bab Ballads* demonstrate, with a particular interest in costume, another link with his predecessor, Planché.

That Gilbert exercised his prerogative down to the last detail is clear from his reference to an ill-advised chorister in a revival of *Trial by Jury*:

> There is a man in the chorus named Moss, a 'funny' man who is the bane of true comic opera. He has overacted right through rehearsals and, although I told the 'jurymen' not to make up with wigs etc., he nevertheless took upon himself to appear last night in a grotesque flaxen wig. . . . I suggest that he be put in the back row at the end furthest from the stage — then his exaggerations will not be import-ant.[8]

Gilbert's clashes with his principals, particularly over gagging onstage and gadding offstage, have often been related. His sustained contribution to the rise of the author-producer consolidated the earlier work of Planché, Boucicault, and Robertson. His example was followed by Pinero, whose handling of his problem plays in the 1890s was marked by complete and rigid command of detail, and by Shaw in the next decade. It was an approach well suited to the elaborate forces of the musical stage, less happily applied to naturalism. Shaw was in the habit of calling his work: 'grand opera without the music', a significant comment on his debt to Gilbert the producer.

The steadily evolving form of the Savoy Operas liberated Gilbert from many of the restrictions that had cramped his earlier work at the Haymarket. The switch from blank verse in the fairy plays (or rhyming couplets in burlesque) to prose enabled his true voice to be heard. It had the measured cadences of a lawyer, but a lawyer with a sense of fun, who saw much to amuse him in the contrast between the ritual of the law-court or theatre and the reality of the world beyond. Reversion in *Princess Ida* to blank verse derived from the earlier *Princess* illustrated the gap between an imitated and an individual idiom. Casting off the ready-made melodies of his early burlesques also fostered the genuinely lyrical gifts he possessed. Although he became known chiefly for his patter-songs, he was often best when briefest.

True there is no substantial change in his character-drawing between the plays and operas. The predatory spinster figures as prominently in *The Pirates of Penzance* or *Patience* as in *Tom Cobb* or *Foggerty's Fairy*. The supreme confidence of the juvenile remains.

Maggie Macfarlane in *Engaged* consults her mirror and tells Cheviot Hill:

> Oh, sir, can I close my een to the picture that my looking-glass holds up to me twenty times a day? . . . Why, sir, it wad just be base ingratitude! No, it's best to tell the truth about a' things: I am a varra, varra, beautiful girl!

Yum-Yum is of exactly the same opinion:

> Yes, I am indeed beautiful! . . . Can this be vanity? No! Nature is lovely and rejoices in her loveliness. I am a child of Nature, and take after my mother.

But the wider context and more varied subject-matter of the operas soften the focus and divert attention from the relentless self-seeking of the earlier characters. There is even a touch of geniality in the portrayal of some of the older generation: Little Buttercup is 'a plump and pleasing person', the Lord Chancellor 'a clean old gentleman'. The Duke of Plaza-Toro has an unexpected humility which is all the more fetching for being tongue-in-cheek. 'Take her' he tells his daughter's suitor, 'and may she make you happier than her mother has made me — if possible'. In a similar situation in *Engaged* Symperson's comment is: 'Oh Lor'! Poor Cheviot! Dear me, it don't bear thinking of!'

By focussing on institutions (the Law, the Royal Navy, the House of Lords, government in many aspects and fancy dresses) or movements (Aestheticism, Women's Education) Gilbert was also able to divert the searching light he threw in his Haymarket plays on individual selfishness and deceit. The importance of his 'homogeneous' chorus in this change of emphasis is apparent. It has been plausibly argued[9] that the function of the chorus is to convert the action into a species of ritual. They intrude on an unfamiliar world and upset its conventions and values, producing an imbroglio only soluble by one of Gilbert, the ex-barrister's, legal fictions. Since the laws of comic opera lay down that love must find a way, a sacrificial victim is often needed, either to enter into a marriage of convenience (Koko, Dick Dauntless, Phoebe Meryll), or face a lonely future (Bunthorne, Jack Point), or literally go to Hell (John Wellington Wells).

While it is clear that the avenging hand of authority shows itself in the person of the Mikado or the structure of the Tower, both somewhat frightening forms for comic opera, nevertheless Gilbert's tone is mostly good-humoured. Fantasy and solid sense coexist happily in the Savoy Operas, whose frontiers are accurately defined by the synopsis of scenery in *Iolanthe*:

> *Act One:* An Arcadian Landscape.
> *Act Two:* Palace Yard, Westminster (with a real life Guardsman to keep the peace and oblige the Fairy Queen).

There is always a strong underswell of belief in the very institutions Gilbert ridicules, a belief the Savoy audiences shared heartily. In this respect apparently satiric strokes like 'He is an Englishman!' or 'When Britain really ruled the waves' are ultimately reassuring, not contemptuous, and the very occasional lapse (such as the 'Dickensian realism' of Strephon's song 'Fold your flapping wings' or Robin's 'Uncommonly dear at the price') recognised as such and deleted. The sheer preposterousness of most of the denouements, pushing legal fiction to absurdity, reinforces the overall impression of make-believe.

Sullivan's contribution to the softening of the character-drawing and to the sustained enchantment of the atmosphere was enormous. Without its elegiac setting Lady Jane's 'Sad is that woman's lot' in *Patience* would be a sad lot indeed. But the composer was capable of enhancing many kinds of lyric, not merely the satiric. He was probably least successful in his handling of the romantic ballad — his idea of the sentimental coincided with rather than complemented Gilbert's, and the result was often undistinguished, as in Alexis' songs in *The Sorcerer* or Margaret's 'Only Roses'. But his ensemble writing grew in stature — as a comparison of any of the early Act Two Finales with those of *The Yeomen of the Guard* or *The Gondoliers* demonstrates. Less obviously he could raise the theatrical tension where the libretto called for it but the librettist was struggling. Gilbert's comment that he 'had hoped the scene would be treated more humorously'[10] (of the materialisation of the Ancestors in *Ruddigore*) is a much quoted example. Briefer but no less successful is Iolanthe's apparent sacrifice of her life to ensure her son's happiness, where to the none-too-promising words: 'Aiaiah! Aiaiah!

86

Willaloo!' the offstage chorus provides real poignancy and a sense of doom. The comparison with Selene's abasement in *The Wicked World* is instructive.

Indeed Sullivan saved *The Yeomen of the Guard* from the ineffectiveness that marked Gilbert's version of the Faust story, *Gretchen*. The setting and plot of *The Yeomen* precluded fantasy; the attempt to suggest period robbed Gilbert of his personal idiom (as earlier *Dan'l Druce, Blacksmith* at the Haymarket — a play of the 'second person singular variety' — had done). But Sullivan responded gladly to its call for both brilliance and pathos. After the first night he noted in his diary:

> I was awfully nervous and continued so until the duet 'Heighday' which settled the fate of the Opera. Its success was tremendous; 3 times *encored*! After that everything went on wheels . . .[12]

Everything also went on wheels in the writing of *The Gondoliers* which followed, and which the composer described in a letter to his partner as 'a perfect book'.[13] Victorian Venice suited Gilbert's style in a way that Tudor England did not. The libretto is uncharacteristic (which is perhaps what appealed to Sullivan), lacking Gilbert's special brand of fantasy or even irony except of the gentlest, but its proportions are admirable, its characters genially presented, and its tone consistently sunny without being smug. Sullivan responded with his happiest score, and the piece might (with a look towards its less inspired successor) be subtitled *Utopia Unlimited,* rather than *The King of Barataria.*

The Savoy Operas combined with Irving's productions at the Lyceum to establish the theatrical tone of the 1880s. In each case a hitherto suspect form of entertainment — melodrama and operetta — had been shown to be acceptable, even highly desirable. The proof of this claim was the preponderance of women in the audience. Throughout the Victorian period there was a strong presumption that unescorted females at the theatre were there to sell themselves — a belief that activated Mrs Ormiston Chaunt in her campaign against the Empire Promenade as late as 1894.[14] But even respectable houses had difficulty in drawing a gentlewoman without male escort. If Queen Victoria, eager playgoer as she had been until her husband's death, totally foreswore visits to the theatre for the rest of her life, her subjects would certainly think twice about the matter. One important innovation which the Lyceum and the Savoy pioneered was the regular matinee, then and since a largely female preserve. Though the Bancrofts and others in the 1870s had offered occasional 'morning performances' of particular successes, the scheduling of regular matinees was made possible by the greatly increased interest women took in the theatre.

A clear manifestation of this was the amount of space now devoted in the press to fashions on and off the stage. 'A Lady Correspondent' wrote ecstatically if inappropriately about the 'Pretty Dresses at the Premiere' of Irving's *Lear*, where 'pale pink was evidently the popular colour for cloaks, and it was equally effective in cloth or brocade'.[15] Of the production itself the article asserted rashly that 'the costumes were perfectly correct and no modern colours appeared in the dresses'. 'Mildred' of the London *Figaro* was on more recent and safer ground when describing the Professional Bridesmaids in *Ruddigore*:

> So tasteful, so delicate, so harmonious, that if ever I raved about anything, I should be tempted to rave about them. Some of them were soft, fairy-like tints that it is hard to find a name for. But it seems to me that the twenty-four frocks included every sweetly delicate hue an imaginative colourist can fancy, from jonquille to blush pinks, from tender apple green to soft pearl grey, from primrose to fawn.[16]

One significant feature of performances at the Savoy copied from Continental houses and missing from the Lyceum, was the printed text in the hands of many of the audience, a subject of much mirth then and since, with accounts of 'swishing sounds' as the spectators turned over a page simultaneously. Such a ritual contributed to the idea, regularly advanced, of Gilbert and Sullivan opera as a religion: this practice, together with the Gallery's partiality for singing 'Hail Poetry!' or 'I hear the soft note'[17] on opening nights do smack of prayer and psalm, and seem worlds away from the outcry at the Bancrofts' abolition of the Haymarket Pit.

At the Lyceum there was insufficient light in the auditorium to read the play as it progressed, even if a text had been published, which — outside Shakespeare — Irving mostly declined to do. The different practices of the two theatres underline the distinction between their policies: the Lyceum offered Irving and Terry in an absorbing theatrical experience; the Savoy employed a highly trained, semi-permanent company, but its success was based on the qualities of text and score, to which the demand not only for the libretto but, in an age of 'Sing-and-play-it-yourself', even more strongly for the sheet-music testified. In this respect the Gilbert and Sullivan operas provided what no other management of the period could offer: a library of theatrical works which existed outside the theatre, establishing their perennial appeal by their availability to a public without regular access to the theatre. The popularity of the Savoy Operas in performance, both professional and amateur, since the original productions, is a tribute to their theatrical vitality; but the eagerness with which the texts have been and are studied, and the regularity with which the music is heard (enormously increased by twentieth-century aids) attests their intellectual and artistic value.

The history of Gilbert and Sullivan, first at the Opera Comique and from 1881 at D'Oyly Carte's own theatre, the Savoy, makes an interesting comparison with the fortunes of the theatre at which they first worked together. The Gaiety, though by no means exclusively a burlesque house, did place its 'sacred lamp' conspicuously outside the theatre and on the stage. As such its audience was quite distinct from the Savoy's, with a strong masculine emphasis in the auditorium and a strong feminine emphasis onstage. Like D'Oyly Carte, John Hollingshead recruited and nursed a group of resident artistes, including Nellie Farren (a successor to Marie Wilton in 'boy' roles), Edward Terry (later a leading exponent of farce), Kate Vaughan, and Edward Royce, known between them in the 1870s as the 'Gaiety quartet'. Though Hollingshead employed authors nurtured in the 'travesty' tradition, like H.J. Byron, Burnand, and Robert Reece, there was a growing shortage of obvious targets, as theatrical taste grew more refined. Some of the titles, such as *Gulliver's Travels*, *Monte Cristo Junior*, and *Carmen Up-to-Date*, indicate how far it was necessary to cast the net in order to make a catch. Where a contemporary success was selected, the tormented title (*The Vicar of Wide-Awake-Field; or, The Miss Terry-ous Uncle*) suggests a struggle to fit it into burlesque form.

The Gaiety therefore turned increasingly to those fairy-tale subjects which had made their appearance in extravaganza some forty years earlier, but were now also raided for pantomime: notably

89

*Cinderella, Aladdin,* and *The Forty Thieves,* and there was a substantial exchange of artistes between music-hall, pantomime, and burlesque. Another sign of the times was the extension to full length of the later Gaiety burlesques, starting with *The Forty Thieves* in 1880, a further step away from the assorted fare of the mid-Victorian bill. These full-length burlesques were chiefly designed to show off the talents of Nellie Farren and later Fred Leslie, who first appeared at the Gaiety in 1885, the same year that D'Oyly Carte's assistant, George Edwardes, moved across from the Savoy, replacing Hollingshead the following season. Fred Leslie retains a modest niche in theatrical history for his mimicry (in ballet-skirt) of Irving, introduced into *Ruy Blas; or, the Blasé Roué* (1889). Irving complained, and the Lord Chamberlain silenced Leslie (though he did not succeed in suppressing the imitation which was continued in mime), but this many-sided performer, reminiscent of Frederick Robson, deserved more than a gleam of reflected glory.

Each theatre had its own public, and if the appeal of Gilbert and Sullivan diverted theatregoers to the Savoy, it was not the burlesque audience but the operatic which suffered, as the fate of the former Italian Opera reveals. After a fire in 1867, the new Her Majesty's remained unopened for five years, then endured a chequered history of visiting companies, both operatic and dramatic, 'Haverley's American United Mastodon Minstrels', and *Uncle Tom's Cabin.* In 1891 the building was demolished, to rise again at the bidding of Beerbohm Tree. It seems clear that the appeal of comic opera had much to do with these vagaries.

However appealing, comic opera could not reproduce itself indefinitely. As long as Gilbert and Sullivan collaborated successfully (if not always happily), the Savoy's fortunes prospered. But as early as 1886 Edwardes tried out a musical play, *Dorothy,* with a score by Sullivan's right-hand man, Alfred Cellier. It did not find favour at the Gaiety, and Edwardes let it go out of his hands, to the Prince of Wales's; it ultimately ran for 931 performances. The new decade brought difficulties for both the Savoy and the Gaiety. The estrangement of Gilbert and Sullivan between *The Gondoliers* and *Utopia Limited* left D'Oyly Carte struggling for substitutes. At the Gaiety a declining taste for burlesque was sadly accelerated by the retirement of Nellie Farren in 1891 and the premature death of Fred Leslie in 1892. It was evident that a new formula was needed.

This formula, later hailed as 'musical comedy', emerged only gradually. It employed many of the performers and devices of burlesque, and exposed the ladies of the chorus as fully as ever. But it discarded the 'travesty' approach, and particularly burlesque costumes with their bizarre mixture of styles, in favour of contemporary clothes and settings.[18] Edwardes's first experiment in this style, *In Town* (1892), was staged at the Prince of Wales's. It retained strong associations with the theatrical subject-matter of burlesque (the chorus represented 'Ladies of the Ambiguity Theatre'), but achieved enough identity of its own to be recognised as a new departure, and was transferred to the Gaiety. A further break with tradition occurred after the failure of one of the Gaiety's old favourites, *Little Jack Shepherd*, when revived in 1894. It was succeeded by *The Shop Girl*, the first full-grown musical comedy to open there. Henceforward the emphasis in Edwardes's work fell more on the music, by composers like Ivan Caryll, Sidney Jones, and Lionel Monckton, who did not aim as high as Sullivan but pleased more widely, and 'smart' rather than broad comedy. His success enabled him to extend to other theatres, notably the Prince of Wales's (where perversely *A Gaiety Girl* had already been staged in 1893), and Daly's, opened by an American, Augustin Daly, for another American, Ada Rehan, to play Shakespeare, but now increasingly given over to musical plays.

It was against this background that D'Oyly Carte managed to bring together Gilbert and Sullivan for *Utopia Limited* and three years later *The Grand Duke*. But whatever the merits and demerits of these two works, time and taste had begun to pass their writers by. A reversal was taking place in the roles of straight and musical theatre. With Hare, the Kendals, and Wyndham, 'legitimate' drama had been mostly French adaptation, acceptable in performance but lacking staying power or native strength. The Savoy Operas had provided the public with precisely what the St James's or Criterion denied them: a truly English entertainment, written for and by Englishmen of intelligence and taste. But in the new decade a dramatic renaissance was under way, and actor-managers, old and new, began to call on English playwrights to challenge the Sardous, Meilhacs and Halévys.

This challenge was successfully answered. 'Society drama', serious in tone, English in origin, increasingly held the stages of the Haymarket, the Criterion, and the St James's. An audience faced with problem plays in the legitimate theatre looked for less taxing entertainment from the musical stage. It welcomed *A Gaiety Girl* and *The Geisha* as a relaxing alternative to *Patience* or *The Mikado*. D'Oyly Carte struggled to fill the Savoy with Gilbert and Sullivan in revival, and searched for substitutes, employing such unlikely talents as J.M. Barrie, Conan Doyle, and Pinero. None proved gifted in this field, but their aptitudes were really immaterial. The originality of comic opera was exhausted.

NOTES

1  J.R. Planché, *Extravaganzas* (1879), Vol. II, p. 66.
2  *Report of the Select Committee on Theatrical Licences and Regulations* (1866), pp. 59-60.
3  See Jane W. Stedman, *Gilbert before Sullivan* (1967), *passim*.
4  T. Edgar Pemberton, *Society* and *Caste* (1905), Introduction, p. xxxi.
5  Jane W. Stedman, 'Gilbert's Stagecraft: Little Blocks of Wood' in *Gilbert and Sullivan*: Papers presented at the International Conference held at the University of Kansas in May 1970, ed. James Helyar (1971), p. 204.
6  Ibid., p. 207.
7  Ibid., p. 204.
8  Ibid., p. 197.
9  e.g. by Max Keith Sutton, *W.S. Gilbert* (1975), pp. 95-96.
10  Letter to A.E.T. Watson, printed in his *Sporting and Dramatic Career* (1918), p. 85.
11  Hesketh Pearson, *Gilbert: His Life and Strife* (1957), p. 64.
12  Herbert Sullivan and Newman Flower, *Sir Arthur Sullivan: His Life, Letters and Diaries* (second edition 1950), p. 181.
13  Ibid., p. 197.
14  See R. Mander and J. Mitchenson, *The Lost Theatres of London* (1968), pp. 73-74.
15  Unidentified cutting in Percy Fitzgerald Collection, Garrick Club, Vol. X, p. 113.
16  Jane W. Stedman, 'Gilbert's Stagecraft', p. 200.
17  François Cellier and C. Bridgeman, *Gilbert, Sullivan, and D'Oyly Carte* (1914), p. 130.
18  R. Mander and J. Mitchenson, *Musical Comedy: A Story in Pictures* (1969), p. 12.

CHAPTER FIVE

# 'Our Little Parish of St James's'

To the casual observer the 1890s may have seemed a decade of consolidation rather than expansion. Though the new theatres built in central London added distinction to the scene — D'Oyly Carte's English Opera House (better known as the Palace), Daly's, the Duke of York's, Wyndham's, and the palatial Her Majesty's — their number was small when compared with the outburst of building in the previous decade. It was the activity within the buildings that characterised the era, and more particularly the spread of actor-managers (often in partnership with their leading ladies) as a standard feature of theatrical enterprise. The scene was still dominated by Irving at the Lyceum, and his knighthood proved both the peak and the half-way point of the decade. Some of his contemporaries were less active. The Bancrofts had retired altogether from management and were seen only briefly on the stage; the same (as far as the London public was concerned) applied to the Kendals.

Two of Irving's rivals, however, not only continued playing but proved more adaptable to the changing conditions. Wyndham, after modulating from daring French farce to old English comedy, found the appropriate key for his maturity in the Society comedies, notably of Henry Arthur Jones but also of authors such as R.C. Carton and Haddon Chambers. The building of Wyndham's Theatre in 1899 (and its survival when the houses once named Terry's, Toole's, and Hicks' have either changed names or disappeared) was a tribute to his skills, both artistic and financial. Hare, having inaugurated the Garrick in 1889, played there with distinction until 1896, and subsequently moved easily between London, the provinces, and North America. If his name is chiefly associated with the more sombre of Pinero's titles (*The Profligate, The Notorious Mrs Ebbsmith*), it should be added that some of his most successful productions looked back to the sweeter and simpler tones of his Robertsonian apprenticeship, notably *A Pair of Spectacles* (1890) by Sydney Grundy, adapted inevitably from the French (*Les Petits Oiseaux* of Labiche and Delacour) but for all that a self-respecting anecdote of the kindly paterfamilias who sees his nearest and dearest in a very different light through his misanthropic brother's spectacles, but is — in every sense — restored to his own.

Of the names new to management, George Alexander and Herbert Beerbohm Tree made the most enduring mark. After a period of mutually valuable service with Irving, Alexander tried out his managerial powers first at the modest Avenue in 1890, and then boldly moved to the St James's in 1891. His theatre was well chosen, for under his direction it took on the appearance and even character of an exclusive St James's Street club, both front-of-house and backstage, where, as W. Bridges-Adams confirmed:

> There was always time for Mrs Evans [the housekeeper] to give a woman's touch to the flowers and the cushions, time enough to set out in the wings the gilt chairs on which the company awaited their cues.[1]

His success was immediate, and with rare exceptions (of which *Guy Domville* is, perhaps unfairly, remembered because its author was Henry James) consistent.

Soon after Alexander set up management at the St James's, an assessment in the *Theatre* by Golding Bright allowed that

> Voice, form, and feature, all are his, if not in ripe perfection, at least in richer measure than any other player of our time enjoys. Add to these a quick intelligence, and in default of a rush of imagination, a supreme capacity for taking pains, and the inventory of the stock-in-trade of the actor is complete.[2]

The reservations are more eloquent than the acknowledgements. There is no mention, for instance, of passion or poetry, and no clear suggestion of humour. The account sums up, with reference to the recent production of *Lady Windermere's Fan*:

> Such is the masterful execution manifest in the production as a whole, so largely does this challenge admiration in excess of the imaginative and creative powers exhibited in Mr Alexander's work as an actor, that I cannot but conceive that his achievements as a manager will far outweigh his triumphs as a player.[3]

Alexander was the perfect chairman of a committee. When Irving died, the profession placed the funeral in Westminster Abbey under his discrete control, though he was twenty years younger than Wyndham, for instance, and had not served Irving half as long as Martin-Harvey. His talent for committee-work (rarely given to men of the theatre) also stood him in good stead when he was elected to the London County Council in 1907. The previous year he had achieved his greatest success in a Pinero play (and one of his and that author's last unqualified triumphs) as Hilary Jesson, the diplomat, in *His House in Order*. A.B. Walkley wrote of this character:

> He loves the sound of his own voice. He is a perfect martyr to dictionary English; even in the most intimate tête-à-tête he is careful to 'admit that your allegations are not unfounded', or to 'point out that matters will eventually adjust themselves'. Well, as he himself would say, God bless him; he represents a little weakness of Mr Pinero's, and so we must accept him with philosophic tolerance. Mr Alexander plays him with manifest gusto; the more wordy the speech the more the actor seems to revel in it. Again, God bless him.[4]

In the years between *Lady Windermere's Fan* and *His House in Order* God did bless Alexander and his theatre. If the Lyceum under Irving was a temple of the arts, the St James's under Alexander was a parish on its best behaviour.

Of all the actors of this period Alexander's name is most closely associated with the fashionable drawing-room drama which he took over from the Kendals amongst others and naturalised. Tree, an altogether more mercurial figure, emerged as an actor in the early

1880s and as a manager (after a spell at the Comedy) when he became director of the hallowed Haymarket in 1887. Although he came to be widely hailed as 'Irving's successor', he was decidedly resistant, both professionally and personally, to classification. While chiefly remembered as a purveyor of 'upholstered' Shakespeare, overset, overdressed, and overpopulated by livestock, yet during his ten years at the Haymarket his record of Shakespeare was modest (*The Merry Wives, Hamlet, Henry IV Part 1*) and his achievements in contemporary drama considerable. He played successfully not only in some less than major pieces by Grundy, Jones, and Haddon Chambers, but achieved popularity in Wilde (*A Woman of No Importance*) and risked unpopularity in Ibsen (*An Enemy of the People*). There is certainly an interesting parallel between Irving's triumph in *The Bells*, on which his regime at the Lyceum was founded, and Tree's in *Trilby*, on which his building of Her Majesty's was financed. The roles of Mathias and Svengali have much in common, including mesmerism and horrific death-throes. But if Tree can be convicted on some charges of outstripping Irving in 'pictorial' Shakespeare, he can also be singled out for a *Hamlet* 'without scenery', and later for a London Shakespeare Festival which by no means glorified the actor-manager alone, since it gave stage-space to some of his rivals (including Bourchier, Lewis Waller, and H.B. Irving) and even artistic foes (Granville Barker, William Poel).[5]

Indeed the leading actor-managers were often more flexible than has been recognised. Alexander was as much a master of costume revels (*The Prisoner of Zenda, Old Heidelberg, If I Were King*) and even of Shakespeare on occasion, as of drawing-room drama, and believed he had found in Stephen Phillips a Shakespeare of the twentieth century. *Paolo and Francesca*, which he staged in 1902, led to several other productions of Phillips's plays, though not to a twentieth-century poetic drama. Wyndham wisely eschewed Shakespeare, but unwisely attempted Cyrano de Bergerac, and found a comparable poetaster to Phillips in Louis Napoleon Parker, whose *Rosemary* and *The Jest* he mounted with varying fortunes.

In between the major figures of this group-portrait can be detected actors who were often highly successful in their own day but not as closely associated with one theatre and therefore not as widely recorded and remembered. Wilson Barrett, whose career stretched back to the 1870s and who rashly tackled *Hamlet* in virtual opposition to Irving in 1884, quitted the Princess's in 1890, but found large audiences elsewhere and suitably flamboyant roles in such pieces as *The Manxman* and above all *The Sign of the Cross*, which he wrote and first presented in London in 1896. Amongst the younger generation Cyril Maude and Winifred Emery took over the Haymarket from Tree; there they played acceptably light comedy, including Barrie (*The Little Minister*), and rehearsed *You Never Can Tell* until Shaw withdrew it rather than himself withdraw from rehearsals. Charles Hawtrey's name was associated with a number of theatres including the Comedy, but effectively with only one kind of easy-going, hard-working entertainment. Arthur Bourchier and his first wife, Violet Vanbrugh, were similarly mobile, though mostly to be found at the height of their success at the Garrick, in drawing-room comedy of a less demanding character than the St James's variety.

Two actor-managers, both connected with Irving's Lyceum, deserve a more detailed account, though for different reasons. Johnston Forbes-Robertson was by no means a pupil of Irving; his career looked back too far. He had supported almost every leading actor in London, including Hare and the Bancrofts, and his appearances with Irving, though crucial, were few (Claudio in *Much Ado*, Buckingham in *Henry VIII*, Sir Lancelot). But it was at the Lyceum in Irving's absence that he made his debut as an actor-manager, and also at the Lyceum when he was forty-four that his Hamlet created an impression as favourable and more lasting than Irving's twenty-five years earlier, above all because in Shaw's words:

> He does not utter half a line; then stop to act; then go on with
> another half line; and then stop to act again, with the clock running
> away with Shakespeare's chances all the time. He plays as Shakes-
> peare should be played, on the line and to the line, with the utterance
> and acting simultaneous, inseparable and in fact identical.[6]

For the same reason he was far more successful than Irving (though almost as old) as Romeo, and equally predictably, he was weak where Irving was weak: in Shakespeare's 'heavies', Macbeth and Othello. His record in contemporary drama was also mixed: he eventually played the vehicle Shaw devised for him, *Caesar and Cleopatra*, but came to grief with a vehicle Jones devised for Irving, *Michael and His Lost Angel.*

Gifted as both player and painter, his was really too delicate a spirit for actor-management, particularly when Mrs Patrick Campbell (whom he loved distractedly) was his leading lady, though he was more fortunate with her successor, the American Gertrude Elliott, whom he married. As the Shakespearean repertory began to elude him, so he turned to Lyceum-type melodrama in plays such as *The Light That Failed* and *The Passing of the Third Floor Back*, in which he was popular but wasted, and knew it. He summed up his own career when at the end of it he declared:

> Never at any moment have I gone on the stage without longing for the moment when the curtain would come down on the last act.[7]

Such were never Irving's sentiments, or those of the other Lyceum graduate who was in every sense a disciple of Irving. John Martin-Harvey served fifteen years' apprenticeship under him, never achieving a lead or even an important supporting role, but loyally filling out those corners allotted him. Then in 1898 he followed Forbes-Robertson into the Lyceum during one of Irving's tours and offered a dramatisation of the Dickens novel Irving had rejected in favour of *The Dead Heart*. Harvey's Sydney Carton in *The Only Way* might be seen as the last manifestation of that important strain in Victorian drama which Dickens represented, even though he was never a recognised dramatist. Its romance, swagger, and pathos established Harvey, less as a London actor-manager than as a touring star who looked in on London, just as his repertoire, a mixture of Shakespeare and melodrama, looked back to the nineteenth century, though he continued to act until 1939. There were splendid if isolated moments, such as his Oedipus at Covent Garden in 1912, but one of his few successful appearances in a recognisably 'modern' play was — significantly — as Dick Dudgeon in *The Devil's Disciple*, Shaw's affectionate tribute to 'Adelphi melodrama'.

Another disciple who served the briefest of apprenticeships with Irving was Frank Benson, Paris in *Romeo and Juliet* but shortly afterwards an actor-manager himself (at twenty-four). He first undertook these duties at the Public Hall, Airdrie, Lanarkshire, and his career was to be spent largely out of London, most beneficially at

Stratford-on-Avon, whose Shakespeare Festivals he supported virtually single-handed from 1886 for the best part of thirty years. In 1900 during one of his infrequent London seasons he offered *Henry V*, which Max Beerbohm reviewed somewhat wrily:

> The fielding was excellent, and so was the batting. Speech after speech was sent spinning across the boundary, and one was constantly inclined to shout: 'Well played, sir! Well played *indeed*!' As a branch of university cricket, the whole performance was indeed beyond praise. But, as a form of acting, it was not impressive.

and concluding:

> I trust that Mr Benson will have a successful season. His enthusiasm for Shakespeare is very laudable and attractive. No one could help wishing him well. But — he really must break himself and his company of this fatal cricketing-habit.[8]

Of course Benson did not — probably could not — give up cricket and temper his ways to his means. But a more professional performer could not have accomplished all he did; it was because he mixed Shakespeare with sport that he could accept the limitations of leading a penurious touring company, and because he was an amateur in the sense of loving the life, that his company and his public loved and followed him.

Bravely as Irving and his disciples continued to provide a theatrical flavour culled from proven recipes, the bill of fare in the 1890s was increasingly characterised by novelty, in particular by English, not French, cooking. The era was marked, after a twenty-year gap following Robertson's death, by the emergence of native playwrights and a recognisably English drama. Two at least of these, Pinero and Jones, had been preparing themselves for such a development, but their work in the 1890s transcended these preparations, and other authors, notably Wilde, turned to the theatre from other fields. Indeed the emergence of an important dramatists' 'school' was as much a professional as a theatrical development. Even before the 1890s the growth of a touring system which showed off and paid off the writer's work more profitably than the old 'stock' system brought great benefit to the playwright's earnings. The passing of the International Copyright Convention of 1887 and the American Act of 1891 extended this benefit. Before the Convention, Jones earned £18,000 from *The Silver King*; after it, *The Second Mrs Tanqueray* brought Pinero £30,000.[9] Sixty years earlier Douglas Jerrold had been paid a lump sum of £60 for *Black-Ey'd Susan*.

Another important consequence was the playwright's freedom to publish his work without jeopardising his copyright. Both Pinero and Jones were quick to take advantage of this by initiating the printing of standard editions of their plays, some of them as much as ten years old but still in manuscript. Pinero pointed out in the introduction to *The Times*, the first of his to appear:

> The publication of plays concurrently with their stage-production, in the exact shape — save for the excision of technical stage-directions — in which they have left the actor's hands, therefore, can hardly fail to be of some value to the English theatre at large.[10]

Jones, whose *Saints and Sinners* appeared at the same time, went further:

> If, from this time forward, a playwright does not publish within a reasonable time after the theatrical production of his piece, it will be an open confession that his work was a thing of the theatre merely, needing its garish artificial light and surroundings, and not daring to face the calm air and cold daylight of print.[11]

Thus Archer's plea ten years before for widely available reading editions was increasingly answered; unproduced playwrights had the recourse of printing where managers rejected, as Shaw rapidly showed; and novelists like Barrie, Hall Caine, Maugham, and later Galsworthy and Bennett were encouraged to write for both publics. Indeed the changed circumstances may even have diverted Pinero from challenging Meredith or Jones from copying Hardy.

These circumstances certainly altered the locales depicted within the proscenium. Just as the stiff dress-shirts and fashionable gowns had distinguished audiences in the 1880s, so now managers and authors conspired to make the stage mirror the stalls, with settings of Mayfair drawing-rooms or elegant country-seats, and lists of characters inspired by Debrett. Self-respecting drama, it was agreed, demanded people of independent means, living, like John Worthing and Aubrey Tanqueray, in Albany, or owning a house in Belgrave

Square 'let by the year to Lady Bloxham', with rural retreats at 'Willowmere' or even 'the Sporran, Fifeshire, N.B.'. Those responsible for selecting these confidence-inspiring addresses, persuaded themselves it was necessary on literary grounds. Pinero, for example, suggested to Archer:

> I think you would find, if you tried to write drama, not only that wealth and leisure are more productive of dramatic complications than poverty and hard work, but that if you want to get a certain order of ideas expressed or questions discussed, you must go pretty well up the social scale. . . . You must take into account the inarticulateness, the inexpressiveness, of the English lower-middle and lower classes — their reluctance to analyse, to generalise, to give vivid utterance to their thoughts or their emotions.[12]

Where Pinero practised what he preached here, the result could be unfortunate. In *The Princess and the Butterfly* (1897), a play with a most exclusive personnel, both playwright and public found little interest in whether the Princess of Pannonia married her middle-aged admirer ('the Butterfly') or her young protegé. But in fact Pinero did not conform to his own dictum. There was articulateness and expressiveness in the 'theatricals' of *Trelawny of the Wells*, in the manicurist who challenged Lord Quex, in the money-conscious manufacturers of *The Thunderbolt*. It took time and effort for him to adjust from the professional worlds of his best Court farces to the aristocratic atmosphere of his St James's plays. Moving from farce to problem play by way of satire put various pitfalls in his path. The crudely drawn gentry of *The Cabinet Minister* or *The Times* seem greatly inferior artistically, though not socially, to the magistrates, clergymen, and schoolteachers who preceded them.

New themes as well as unfamiliar people also proved intractable to Pinero's pen. *The Weaker Sex* (written five years before its production in 1889) attempts the topical issue of Women's Rights but in a wholly flippant tone, as exhibited in the following exchange:

MRS BOYLE-CHEWTON: Why can't women vote?
LORD GILLINGHAM:     They can — they tell the men how to.
MRS BOYLE-CHEWTON: Why can't women sit?
LORD GILLINGHAM (*puzzled*): They can — can't they?

Pinero's most recent champion defends this treatment on the grounds that the playwright 'used the women's rights movement not as the subject of the play . . . but topically'.[13] The fact remains that, having drawn attention to it in the title, he proceeded to set up a skittle-alley of feminists, only to knock them down to provide easy fun. Both Pinero and Jones seemed on occasion to be vying with Gilbert in attempting satire, and both lost by the comparison.

While adjusting somewhat painfully to the demands of drawing-room drama, Pinero explored more profitably the sentimental vein of *The Squire*. The longest run of any of his plays was achieved by *Sweet Lavender*, with 684 performances at Edward Terry's Theatre from 1888. The author dismissed it as a pot-boiler. 'They can adapt *Sweet Lavender* till it is sage and onions for all I care' he told Henry Arthur Jones,[14] and much of it was in the outmoded style of Robertson or even H.J. Byron. But there are touches of genuine humanity in the ageing barber, Bulger's, devotion to Lavender's mother:

> I was the first wot ever put scissors to your Lavender's silky head, Mrs Rolt . . . And I've had the 'andlin' of your tresses too — ay, and the singein' of 'em — till I found I loved you too fond to do your 'air what I call justice. (*Gloomily offering his verses*) And now it's come down to poetry. . . . It ain't much good, but intellectually it's my all, ma'am.

Terry's own part as a broken-down barrister, struggling between his addiction to the bottle and his devotion to his friends, commands both pathos and comedy, suggesting Tom Wrench twenty years on, with his dramatic masterpieces still unproduced. For *Trelawny of the Wells*, in which Pinero returned to his sentimental strain after a prolonged spell of problem plays, is the climax of his work in this vein, if not the summit of his whole achievement. The theatrical world suits his 'heavyweight' dialogue perfectly, and the contrast between the rowdy warmth of the Wells and the austere calm of Cavendish Square is precisely judged. Although an actor and playwright, Pinero can stand back and assess his subject. In particular, he never overcalls the claims of the Wrench/Robertson school of reform, indebted to it as he was. When the superannuated manager of the Wells finds himself assigned by the new wave to the role of 'an old, stagey, out-of-date actor' and his wife banished to the wardrobe, Pinero reminds himself that problem plays will also grow out-of-date:

> TELFER: And so this new-fangled stuff, and these dandified people,
>   are to push us, and such as us, from our stools!
> MRS TELFER: Yes, James, just as some other new fashion will, in
>   course of time, push *them* from their stools.

With commendable restraint he even leaves the audience to create their own first night of Tom Wrench's masterpiece, *Life*, and to determine the future lives of Rose Trelawny and her new leading man.

Between the pot-boiling of *Sweet Lavender* and the artistry of *Trelawny of the Wells* Pinero's career had been transformed, and the three plays Hare presented during his management of the Garrick were greatly influential in this transformation. The second was less crucial to this process, though not without merit. *Lady Bountiful* (1891) also mixes two worlds, in this case the affluence of the land-owning Brents and the tough existence at the 'Hyde Park Riding Academy' of the Dickensian Veale family. The combination, which depends on the plausibility of a hero with a foot in both stirrups, makes an uneasy ride, not least in the dangerous death-scene of the Veale daughter.

*The Profligate*, with which Hare inaugurated his management, was in every respect the more significant play. It is chiefly cited for the manager's insistence on replacing Pinero's ending (the profligate husband's suicide) by a reconciliation between him and his wronged wife. Further-reaching elements were the introduction of Pinero's most uncompromising portrait of an aristocrat and of a 'woman with a past'. Lord Dangars is 'a dissipated-looking man of about forty, dressed in the height of fashion', which suggests *Ruddigore* rather than a problem play, but the author's sharply-focussed portrait and Hare's precise performance placed him convincingly. Janet Preece is far more conventionally drawn, the victim of the Dangars code, though seduced by the husband. Yet it was the 'woman with a past' who proved the fulcrum of most problem plays, Pinero's in particular, but also Wilde's, one of Jones's major successes, and several by secondary writers, in the decade which followed.

The prominence of these fatal females in the 'serious' drama of the 1890s was the subject of much criticism, sometimes ribald, sometimes swingeing. Shaw, whose appearance in the dramatic columns of the *Saturday Review* in 1895 was the turning-point for the theatrically rebellious, was particularly outspoken:

> It may seem strange, even monstrous that a man should feel a constant attachment to the hideous witches of *Macbeth*, and yet yawn at the prospect of spending another evening in the contemplation of a beauteous young leading lady with voluptuous contours and longlashed eyes, painted and dressed to perfection in the latest fashions. But this is just what happened to me in the theatre.
>
> I did not find that matters were improved by the lady pretending to be 'a woman with a past', violently oversexed, or the play being called a problem play, even when the manager, and sometimes, I suspect, the very author, firmly believed the word problem to be the latest euphemism for what Justice Shallow called a *bona roba*, and certainly would not either of them have staked a farthing on the interest of a genuine problem.[15]

Reviewing *The Notorious Mrs Ebbsmith* (the third of Hare's productions of Pinero at the Garrick) shortly after his debut as a dramatic critic, he concluded: 'To tell the truth I disliked the play so much that nothing would induce me to say anything good of it.'[16]

Yet the playwrights' tactics did not derive solely from the commercial considerations Shaw imputed to them. Their stress on female reputation in High Society arose from the restrictions placed on women in that society. Given marriage and motherhood as their only occupation, to be compromised, however slightly, was social suicide. Discovery in a bachelor's chambers late at night signified 'a fate worse than death' for the 'good' woman, especially if hatless and so constructively flagrante delicto. Until a career outside the home was opened to them, the ambitious were confronted with the choice of dwindling into a wife or living in sin, as Paula Tanqueray demonstrated with Hugh Ardale amongst others. The same choice awaited the working girl who rejected factory or domestic servitude, supplying Shaw himself with the subject-matter of *Mrs Warren's Profession*.

The discrimination between compromised women and compromising men, though manifestly unjust, was an accurate reflection of the divorce laws, which until 1923 offered a husband freedom on the grounds of his wife's adultery but insisted on an additional reason (mostly cruelty or desertion) before freeing a wife. This dual morality, which made Paula a social outcast but Hugh Ardale an acceptable suitor for any other girl than Paula's step-daughter, was by no means a theatrical convention but a harsh fact of marital life. What did give the 'woman with a past' an extra dimension for the playgoer was the lure of the demi-mondaine portrayed by so dazzling a personality as Mrs Patrick Campbell or Marion Terry. To many stall-occupants, particularly female, Paula Tanqueray and Mrs Erlynne were as near they came to meeting a 'fallen' woman, and the encounter had all the fascination of forbidden fruit.

With a genre as strictly conformist as the drawing-room drama of the 1890s it is difficult to distinguish between attitude and treatment. Pinero in particular has been the victim, as much of his admirers as his critics, for the emphasis on construction ('tactics' in his own phrase) which they placed often obscured his sympathies. The stress laid by William Archer on Pinero's exposition without recourse to soliloquy or aside seems excessive to the modern practitioner, who is willing and often committed to acknowledge the audience's presence and the actor's artifice. The opening of *The Second Mrs Tanqueray*, in which Aubrey explains his marriage plans to two friends (subsequently dismissed from the play) and then withdraws 'to write some letters' whilst they in turn explain the position to a newcomer, was judged 'admirable' by William Archer,[17] but is no longer admired. Indeed the play as a whole has suffered from the claims made on its behalf: to Archer it represented 'a new milestone on the path of progress';[18] to the author's American editor it 'revolutionised the English theatre and established in a single night the undeniable existence of a modern English drama'.[19] Without jumping into deep Continental waters and citing *A Doll's House* or *Ghosts*, the chronicler might still point out that *Lady Windermere's Fan* preceded *Mrs Tanqueray* at the St James's by more than a year.

What did single out Pinero's play was not its 'tactics' but its 'strategy' (another of Pinero's own terms), or intent. Believing the time ripe to discard the compromise reached over *The Profligate*, he insisted on Paula's suicide as the inevitable outcome. Even so, he envisaged only a few matinee performances, until a managerial emergency pushed it into a full-scale production and extraordinary success. Nor was its singularity limited to the outcome; useful as the sub-plot (or more accurately parallel-plot) of the Orreyeds proved, it was the fairness of the viewpoint which distinguished this play from its fellows. Aubrey is allowed to denounce 'a man's life' in which he as much as Ardale has been implicated as responsible for Paula's death and the disgrace of her kind, but the raisonneur is allotted the counter-argument:

> AUBREY: To you, Cayley, all women who have been roughly treated, and who dare to survive by borrowing a little of our philosophy, are alike. You see in the crowd of the Ill-used only one pattern; you can't detect the shades of goodness, intelligence, even nobility there. Well, how should you? The crowd is dimly lighted! And besides, yours is the way of the world.
> DRUMMLE: My dear Aubrey, I *live* in the world.
> AUBREY: The name we give our little parish of St James's.
> DRUMMLE: And are you quite prepared, my friend, to forfeit the esteem of your little parish?

As his career progressed, Pinero stretched his canvas wider than this 'little parish', and his centre of interest beyond the woman with a past, her admirers and detractors. Letty Shell, in the play that bears her first name (1903), is a shop-girl, tempted by the advances of a wealthy married man but settling for marriage to a photographer. *The Thunderbolt* takes place in a Midland town, peopled by less than lovely characters. Even *Iris* (1901), though as elegantly set as any drawing-room drama of the period, centres not on a woman with a past but a widow whose tastes are more luxurious than her means, and whose weakness, not her sexuality, proves her downfall.

Pinero resolutely disclaimed the influence of Ibsen on his work, and for an author writing regularly for the St James's and its 'parishioners', this was a necessary precaution. But undoubtedly he set himself a goal comparable to that Ibsen's admirers bespoke for their idol. Seriousness so completely characterised his plays of the 1890s that he lost his farcical touch altogether, and a return to that style for *A Wife without a Smile* (1904) proved a farce without a laugh. It is possible to measure both the achievements and limitations of his serious vein by setting Paula Tanqueray, destroyed by the return to her life of Hugh Ardale, beside Hedda Gabler, ruined by her involvement past and present with Eilert Lövborg. Even more revealing is the parallel between Agnes Ebbsmith's relations with Lucas Cleeve and those of Rebecca West with John Rosmer. Despite

Shaw's scorn, *The Notorious Mrs Ebbsmith* was an ambitious attempt to portray an 'independent woman. Agnes is no 'kept' mistress; after a wretched marriage she has offered her love and care to the young politician whose own marriage and career are in ruins. Like Rebecca she comes to see partnership without passion as a delusion, and her entry 'handsomely gowned, her throat and arms bare' is as much an acknowledgement of this as Rebecca's appearance in her dressing-gown. The denouement of Pinero's play, with the much criticised bible-burning, the unlikely outcome of Agnes's encounter with Cleeve's wife, and the lamely contrived ending, has none of the tragic intensity of *Rosmersholm,* but the parallels exist.

Where this new 'seriousness' did handicap Pinero was in the less ambitious pieces he wrote alongside the problem plays. *The Benefit of the Doubt* (1895) contains the same meticulous plotting, but the tactics of its crucial second act suggest the strategy of a bedroom-farce. A jealous wife contrives to overhear her supposed rival under considerable stress make overtures to the husband, while the rival's own relations wait out of earshot to 'rescue' her. Feydeau would have extracted huge if harsh laughter from such a situation; Pinero in his solemn mood demands sympathy for characters he has not endowed with sufficient redeeming qualities.

*The Gay Lord Quex* (1899) posits a comparable situation actually in a bedroom, that of the Duchess to whom Quex is paying his last respects before marrying the innocent young foster-sister of Sophy Fullgarney, a manicurist who plots to spoil the match by posing as the Duchess's maid and denouncing Lord Quex's morals. Instead she is herself in danger of being exposed, until her unselfishness earns Quex's admiration and mercy. But in the comparable test of the bride-to-be's old flame, the flame proves a flirt and match-making Sophy blesses the Lord and the young lady. Again, for an amoral farce, the tactics (particularly the suspenseful bedroom scene) presage victory. In a morally committed drama the strategy invites defeat.

Pinero's career continued for many years after the death of Irving, the actor-manager under whom he had first served, reaching its high point in 1906 with the enormous success of *His House in Order* (a skeleton-in-the-cupboard story with more than the 'skeleton' in common with Daphne du Maurier's *Rebecca*) and his knighthood — the first conferred on a 'straight' dramatist — in 1909. On either side of this triumph were two failures, *The Thunderbolt* (1908) and *Mid-Channel* (1909), neither well suited to the St James's 'parishioners', the first being too provincial and the second too sombre. To today's playgoer Pinero's name stands for the magician who conjured up the Court farces and warmed the heart with *Trelawny of the Wells*. To the theatre historian he remains the pioneer who wrote *The Second Mrs Tanqueray*. Whether as magician, heart-warmer, or pioneer, his was no mean achievement.

In some accounts of English literature Pinero and Henry Arthur Jones appear as the Beaumont and Fletcher of Victorian drama, their names inseparable, their work unseparated. In fact they never collaborated, and their careers were largely complementary. Whereas Pinero served his apprenticeship chiefly in high-class theatres like the Court and the St James's under Hare and the Kendals, Jones spent the first ten years of his career assembling melodramas for popular audiences, such as Wilson Barrett's at the Princess's. When both found fame and fortune, it was for different managements and in styles differing from their apprentice work, Pinero being closely connected with Alexander and Hare in a series of problem plays of decidedly solemn tone, while Jones wrote most successfully for Wyndham at the Criterion and in an increasingly light-hearted vein. With Wilde they constituted the spearhead of the attack on French adaptations which distinguished the 1890s. Yet of these three Jones's reputation has suffered most. Because he worked unstintingly for the recognition of the theatre as an art and the dramatist as an artist, he exposed himself to charges of failing to practise what he preached, but in fact his achievements were considerable. He was above all prolific and versatile; in the 1890s alone he wrote seventeen produced plays as well as several left unperformed. Though most closely associated with Wyndham, he worked for virtually every leading actor-manager of his day, except Irving. But then Irving was suspicious of dramatists, especially the aspiring kind.

Jones's call for the elevation of English drama to the level of literature was first made as early as 1883, with a piece in the *Nineteenth Century Review* entitled 'The Theatre and the Mob', and found collected form in two books: *The Renascence of the English Drama* (1895) and *The Foundations of a National Drama* (1913). Not surprisingly his pronouncements occasioned some leg-pulling. *Fun* lived up to its title with a set of verses beginning:

'The Stage has got a mission,
    The Stage has got a call:
That great is its position
    Must be distinct to all.
It gilds the pill of knowledge,
    And sermons finds in stones
To fling at school and college — '
    Says Henry Arthur Jones.

and concluding:

Because he's very moral
    Must cakes and ale decline?
And honey turn to sorrel?
    To vinegar the wine?
Oh! sadly, all too sadly,
    Our latest mentor drones,
He's got the swell-head badly,
    Has Henry Arthur Jones.[20]

In 1883 he staked out his belief that

we are on the threshold, not merely of an era of magnificent spectacular and archaeological revivals, but of a living, breathing drama
— a drama that shall not fear to lay bold and reverent hands on the
deepest things of human life today, and freely expose them, and
shall attempt to deal with the everlasting mysteries of human life as
they appear to nineteenth-century eyes.[21]

Yet like others of his generation and beliefs, he was noticeably
obtuse about the renaissance of European drama, particularly in the
shape of Ibsen. The preface to *The Renascence of the English Drama*
concludes with an attack on the Ibsenite movement, although the
playwright is not named:

It tried to seduce us from our smug suburban villas into all sorts of
gruesome kitchen-middens. Now it does not matter what happens
in kitchen-middens. The dark places of the earth are full of cruelties
and abominations. So are the dark places of the soul. We know that
well enough. But the epitaph — it is already written — on all this
realistic business will be — 'It does not matter what happens in
kitchen-middens.'[22]

109

He even introduced an attack on 'kitchen-middens' into the prologue of his ill-fated verse-drama, *The Tempter* (1893), at the Haymarket, in which Tree as the Devil attempted some sort of riposte to the Lyceum *Faust*:

> Leave for awhile the fret of modern life,
> Its cheap pert aims, delirious unrest;
> Leave social maladies and the lust-pest
> To nature's surgery . . .
> Shut out the reek of this stock-jobbing age,
> Its wan-faced railway herds, its wealth, its illth . . .
> Close eyes. Waken in long past lovely years.
> Waken in Chaucer's England . . .

It should be added that he came, if a little late, to acknowledge his blindness to Ibsen's work. *The Foundations of a National Drama* included a lecture given at Harvard in 1906, which concludes:

> Some tribute may perhaps be offered, belated, but I hope not too late, by those whom his tense and shattering genius has at last conquered, and brought to own with regret that they have in part misjudged, in part under-estimated him.[23]

This is bravely said by a man who in his youth offered a version of *A Doll's House* entitled *Breaking A Butterfly*, with 'Flora' returning to her family, and her husband declaring:

> Nothing has happened, except that Flossie was a child yesterday — today she is a woman.

In his own dedication to the theatre Jones reflected the change in late-Victorian attitudes. Born of a strict Baptist family, the playhouse was firmly barred to him until he came to manhood, yet once within its doors he laboured incessantly not only for his own reputation, but for the reputation of his chosen calling. Success, both financial and artistic, came with the production in 1882 of *The Silver King* (written in collaboration with Henry Herman), which confirmed Wilson Barrett's position as an impersonator of strong melodramatic roles, and brought Jones's work to the attention of no less a judge than Matthew Arnold. Although never a professional critic, Arnold was an earnest supporter of the stage who had been moved by the visit of the Comédie Française to London in 1879 to pass the far-reaching verdict: 'The theatre is irresistible; organise the theatre'. The essay in the *Nineteenth-Century Review* which he concluded so quotably also claimed: 'We in England have no modern drama at all', and it was doubtless the sorrow in such a judgment that led him to conclude of *The Silver King*: 'Instead of giving to their audience transpontine diction and sentiments, Messrs Jones and Herman give them literature.'[24] The compliment was well-meant but ill-judged. *The Silver King* was *not* literature, but a shrewdly calculated melodrama, strongly akin to *The Ticket-of-Leave Man*. The settings had been updated (with a bustling railway station instead of the Bellevue Tea Gardens) and the criminals upgraded — Taylor's were counterfeiters, Jones's diamond-thieves — but both plays centred on a foolish yet innocent man, wrongly condemned for another's crime, who wreaks retribution on his persecutors and achieves domestic happiness at last.

Arnold's well-meant tribute seems to have encouraged Jones's ingrained belief that melodrama and literature were readily compatible. Although he recognised the sensational character of the plays he wrote for Wilson Barrett, he failed to see how often his more ambitious essays were similarly flawed. His advocacy of drama as a worthy companion to fiction or poetry regularly distinguished between art and mere entertainment, and between the art-pleasure and amusement-pleasure at which they were respectively aimed. But it is difficult to see where the entertainment ends and the art begins in a play like *The Dancing Girl* (1891), an enormously successful piece of sensationalism which displayed Tree as the dissolute Duke of Guisebury in the toils of Drusilla Ives, the renegade Quaker girl turned coryphée. Three acts of titillation were hardly redeemed by a fourth of retribution (for Drusilla, taking her wages of sin in New Orleans) and repentance (for the Duke, recuperating amongst his faithful tenants in general and one devoted handmaiden in particular).

Despite the sensationalism of *The Dancing Girl*, Jones's work tended to steer clear of the common ground of much problem drama provided by the woman with a past. One such figure was unquestionably Mrs Dane of *Mrs Dane's Defence*, but her fully deserved acclaim tends to obscure Jones's greater concern with the infatuated male. He himself pointed out

> I have treated the passion of a man's love in a different way and on a different level from any of my brother contemporary English dramatists. I have made it more possessive of a man's whole nature, the dominant motive of his conduct, and the arbiter of his fate.[25]

Certainly half a dozen of his more ambitious plays turn on the devotion of a highly regarded professional man to a woman usually ineligible because married, and often unworthy of his love. The Rev. Judah Llewelyn leads off the procession in the play that bears his name (1890); his disciples included two other clergymen, Philos Ingarfield (in *The Crusaders*) and Michael Feversham (the part Forbes-Robertson took over after Irving rejected it); Dr Lewin Carey in *The Physician* (1897), whose relationship to Edana Hinde foreshadows that of Colenso Ridgeon to Jennifer Dubedat; Lucien Edensor in *The Case of Rebellious Susan*, and Edward Falkner in *The Liars*, amongst others.

Passions as strong as theirs call for poets to define them, but there was little of the poet in Jones. In a telling phrase William Archer summed up this failing by commenting: 'The pity is that the world of his imagination is lime-lit, not sunlit.'[26] Another critic, Joseph Knight, in the preface he supplied for *Michael and His Lost Angel*, suggests 'in some respects the love of Michael Feversham and Audrie Lesden seems to take rank with the masterpieces of human passion',[27] and while rejecting Romeo and Juliet as a comparison, goes on to cite Paris and Helen, Antony and Cleopatra, and Des Grieux and Manon Lescaut. Unhappily, Jones's play simply cannot survive in such company. High as he rated it himself, the strength of feeling between his two lovers is constantly undermined by Audrie's apparent flippancy. She end their first encounter by pleading '*very seductively*', 'Do save me. I'm worth saving', and the scene closes with her kissing his mother's portrait and declaring: 'Your bad angel has kissed your good angel' with 'a mock curtsey to him'. Finally, when their single night of passion has cost him his living and (unaccountably) brought on a fatal consumption in her, she dies jesting:

Hold my hand — Tight! Tight! Oh! don't look so solemn —
(*Begins to laugh, a ripple of bright, feeble laughter, growing louder and stronger, a little outburst then a sudden stop, as she drops dead*)

The seeds of this mismatch between religiosity and melodrama lie much earlier, in *Saints and Sinners* (1884). Here Jones was writing of a world he did know — the Dissenting clergyman and his shop-keeping congregation — but his satiric touch is often painfully clumsy, as in the exchange between two deacons plotting their minister's eviction:

> HOGGARD: Then we understand one another. How sweet it is for brethren to dwell together in unity! It is like the precious oil that poured down Aaron's beard! Mrs Prabble and all the little Prabbles quite well?

Even more damaging is the grafting onto a bold, though crude, attack on a subject virtually untouched in the English theatre of the time a seduction story as old as melodrama itself. The minister's daughter allows herself to be abducted by the nearest army officer, and having failed to achieve respectability, since he is already married, returns to her father, disgrace, and a lingering death. The conclusion was altogether too tough for the play's first audience and rapidly revised (in an interesting pointer to Pinero's experience with *The Profligate*), but the mixture proved unhappily characteristic. Matthew Arnold's comment on *Saints and Sinners* — 'You have remarkably the art — so valuable in drama — of exciting interest and sustaining it'[28] — was nearer the mark than his belief in *The Silver King* as 'literature'. Jones's ability to grasp and maintain the attention continued to grow. But his weakness for oversimplified satire regularly sapped the sound construction of his later work, and he seemed incapable of learning by his mistakes; a crude caricature of an emancipated girl, Sophie Jopp, in *Judah*, was followed by another, Una Dell in *The Crusaders*, and a third, Elaine Shrimpton, in *The Case of Rebellious Susan*, the last being particularly obtrusive in a play of considerable comic impact.

Satire was really outside Jones's range, as *The Crusaders* (1891) sadly demonstrated. This was a cherished project which Jones presented at his own expense, including 'furniture and draperies . . .

made by Messrs William Morris and Company, 449 Oxford Street'. But his treatment of the well-to-do proponents of the 'London Reform League' is as unconvincing as their single specified activity — the establishment of rose-farms in Wimbledon tended by seamstresses from 'the worst sweating-shops in the East End' (who predictably turn out to be unsuitable subjects for transplantation). As in *Saints and Sinners,* several of the busybodies introduced are so heavily handled as to defeat the satiric intention: for example, Burge Jawle, 'the great Pessimist Philosopher', whose pessimism is shown to spring from indigestion — and once again the devotion of the Rev. Philos Ingarfield, the League's moving force and 'a sort of Shelley from Peckham Rye', to a wealthy young widow, strikes an uncomfortably solemn note in the proceedings.

Art and artists was another subject close to Jones's heart, and in *The Triumph of the Philistines* (1895) he sketched a group of provincial shopkeepers akin to the chapel-goers of *Saints and Sinners* in more than their names (Jorgan, Blagg, Wapes, Skewett), although their persecution of the Bohemians in their midst is blunted by the ineffectiveness with which the artistic way of life is presented. Nor is Jones more at ease with farce than satiric comedy. *The Manoeuvres of Jane* (1898), although a popular contribution to Cyril Maude's and Winifred Emery's programme at the Haymarket, compares poorly with *The Schoolmistress,* from which it borrows something of its subject-matter. Pinero's farces at their best are precisely engineered and lubricated with human understanding; the manoeuvres of Jones in this instance are clumsy and wretchedly proportioned. He dealt more confidently with the world of shabby stockbroking and fraudulent bankers in *The Rogue's Comedy* (1896), a skilfully turned tale of an impostor on London Society, as adept at mind-reading as company-flotation. Arnold's recognition of his protegé's 'art of exciting interest and sustaining it' was wholly applicable here.

Though bred well beneath its ranks, Jones proved to have the outsider's gifts of observation and mimicry where Society's conventions and idiom were involved. Perhaps the turning-point of his career can be traced to the year 1894 and to the two plays he contributed to that season's offerings. *The Masqueraders* seems to have been conceived by both the author and the manager, George Alexander, as a successor to *The Second Mrs Tanqueray,* presenting Mrs Patrick Campbell in a cognate role to Paula. Dulcie Larondie is similarly déclassée, if not actually 'fallen', since she has cast off her respectable origins to serve as a barmaid in a country hotel. Her beauty and spirit attract the notice of both a brutish baronet and a dreamy astronomer. She chooses the baronet, but is inevitably ill-treated, and in the crucial gambling scene the astronomer wins Dulcie and her child from her husband. But all resemblance to *The Mayor of Casterbridge* ends here; the astronomer is persuaded by Dulcie's self-righteous sister to provide for but not claim her, because 'the woman who gives herself to another man while her husband is alive betrays her sex, and is a bad woman'. Orthodox morality triumphed; the play was less successful.

But when six months later *The Case of Rebellious Susan* opened at the Criterion, orthodox morality took something of a beating and the box-office won a resounding success. Here the heroine is also married to a brutish husband, but rebels against his infidelities, and in the boldest stroke Jones had yet made proclaims her independence:

> HARABIN (*trying to assume a tone of stern authority*): Where are you going, madam?
> LADY SUSAN (*same tone of extremely calm politeness*): I am going to find a little romance, and introduce it into our married life. (*Going off*)
> HARABIN (*loud, angry*): I forbid you, madam! I forbid you!
> (*Lady Susan, in the most graceful, calm, and polite way, snaps her fingers three times at him, each time with a larger action, then backs out door left, bowing profoundly and politely to him.*)

Between the acts Susan finds her little romance under the Egyptian skies with a dashing young diplomat, and the rest of the play is concerned with her friends' efforts to conceal this episode from her husband. Ultimately the raisonneur of the piece persuades her that though married women cannot claim the freedom to retaliate, they can claim the freedom of Bond Street, and that is enough.

But behind this tame conclusion lay another conflict: between playwright and manager, Charles Wyndham. For Jones had daringly written into his piece another conclusion: in the words of his dedication 'To Mrs Grundy' — 'That as women cannot retaliate openly, they may retaliate secretly — and *lie*'. To Wyndham, with the risqué reputation that *Pink Dominos* brought to the Criterion now twenty years behind him, such a conclusion was unacceptable.

Writing to Jones before rehearsals began, he expostulated:

> I stand as bewildered today as ever at finding an author, a clean-living, clear-minded man, hoping to extract laughter from an audience on the score of a woman's impurity. I can realise the picture of a bad woman and her natural and desirable end being portrayed, but that amusement pure and simple should be expected from the sacrifice of that one indispensable quality in respect for womanhood astounds me. I am equally astonished at a practical long-experienced dramatic author believing that he will induce married men to bring their wives to a theatre to learn the lesson that their wives can descend to such nastiness, as giving themselves up for one evening of adulterous pleasure and then returning safely to their husband's arms, provided they are clever enough, low enough, and dishonest enough to avoid being found out.[29]

The crux of their dispute lay in the recriminatory scene between Lady Susan and her diplomat, in which such exchanges as: 'I should kill myself if anyone knew!' and 'You have never spoken of me — boasted to any of your men friends' pointed up the issue. Jones stood his ground, as the printed text confirms, but the cast were under the manager's control, and in Jones's words:

> You may remember that Susan's husband was unfaithful to her and she said in effect, 'I'll pay you out' and she did! I made very sure that she did, but the actor was a bit delicate with his audiences and refused to utter a few lines that made it clear. So I made it clear by addressing it to Mrs Grundy.[30]

Nevertheless the turning-point had been passed, and after 1894 it was the orthodox morality of *The Masqueraders,* not the rebellious spirit of Lady Susan, that characterised Jones's work, particularly his two enduring plays, *The Liars* (1897) and *Mrs Dane's Defence* (1900). Both are cleverly conceived and finely executed studies of the affluent and aristocratic world he had sketched but not yet mastered in *The Dancing Girl* and *The Bauble Shop.* Both contain one extended and supremely effective scene — in *The Liars* the frantic efforts of Lady Jessica Nepean's friends to conceal from her husband the indiscretion she has committed by supping à deux with an admirer, in *Mrs Dane's Defence* the cross-examination she undergoes at the hands of the lawyer (who is also the adoptive father of her fiancé) as to her real identity and involvement in a half-suspected scandal. Each then slips away into anticlimax as the 'holy pretences' (Jones's words, no longer used satirically) of Victorian morality close in and preserve their own from social suicide, while demanding the sacrifice of happiness.

Such conclusions might be acceptable if (as in Wilde) the playwright was aiming no higher than a clever manipulation of an efficient theatrical formula. What raises these plays above Jones's earlier level, only to let them drop further into disappointment, is the expectation of genuine insight and compassion. At the end of the skilfully orchestrated cover-up in *The Liars*, the subject of the exercise suddenly cracks the veneer of concealment:

> LADY JESSICA (*rises very quietly*): Mr Falkner, tell my husband the truth.
> FALKNER: But, Lady Jessica —
> LADY JESSICA: Yes, if you please — the truth, the whole truth, and nothing but the truth. Tell him all. I wish it.

For an instant it seems that (as in *Rebellious Susan*) the playwright is staking his reputation on a plea for impartiality in judging sexual conduct. But the last act sees Wyndham as raisonneur arguing that

> I've nothing to say in the abstract against running away with another man's wife! There may be planets where it is not only the highest ideal morality, but where it has the further advantage of being a practical way of carrying on society. But it has this one fatal defect in our country today — it won't work!

and Lady Jessica abjectly capitulating:

> LADY JESSICA: I think you're the most horrid man I ever met!
> SIR CHRISTOPHER: Because I've told you the truth.
> LADY JESSICA: Yes, that's the worst of it! It is the truth.

Again in *Mrs Dane's Defence* admiration for the perseverance with which Sir Daniel Carteret winnows truth from fiction in seeking to ensure his adopted son's happiness is checked by his admission that twenty years earlier his bid to entice the boy's mother from her husband was defeated purely by chance. What is more:

> I've been successful and happy after a fashion; but there has never been a moment since I lost her when I wouldn't have cheerfully bartered every farthing, every honour, every triumph I've scored in my profession, to stand again on that platform at Liverpool and know she was coming to me.

Add to these sources of disenchantment, the gross indulgence Jones shows his two raisonneurs by providing each with a companionable widow to make them the happiest of men as the curtain falls, and the sense of manipulation rather than inspiration prevails. Yet both plays are not only confidently told but enhanced by incisive dialogue and a nicely distinguished set of supporting characters. All that is lacking is an assertion of absolute human values. Instead the Susans and Jessicas settle for an outing to the theatre (to see a Jones play?) and supper at the Savoy, while Mrs Dane, her true identity admitted, is driven out of the Garden of Eden and exiled to darkest Devon.

In the decade which followed these successes, Jones showed some awareness of the incompatibility between his expertise and adopted beliefs. Some of his later comedies are altogether lighter in texture and tone: *Whitewashing Julia* (1903), for example, is a comic version of *Mrs Dane's Defence*. Julia Wren *may* have been indiscreetly involved with the Duke of Savona while travelling in Italy, but neither the author nor the Hon. William Stillingfleet holds this against her, and the curtain falls on Julia engaged to her suitor and truth left undisturbed. Another play, *Dolly Reforming Herself* (1908), profitably turns from female adultery to female extravagance, and includes one of Jones's most consummate comic scenes as Dolly's husband sinks ever deeper into the impossible task of unravelling Dolly's debts. But by the date of this play another generation of playwrights had sharpened their skills on Jones's whetstone. A comparison between *Dolly Reforming Herself* and Hubert Henry Davies's *The Mollusc*, or later on between *The Liars* and Maugham's *The Circle*, while the younger men were at the height of their success, could only result in Jones's rejection as a past master, not a present magician.

Soon after he assumed the management of the St James's, Alexander suggested to Oscar Wilde, whose name had never appeared on a British playbill, though comprehensively displayed elsewhere, that he write a play for that theatre. The facility with which Wilde proceeded to write four successful comedies in three years is often cited as evidence of his need for money, just as his use of the Sardou *pièce bien faite* as the frame for his paradoxes, already well aired in public and print, is quoted as illustrating his laziness. Wilde's brief but brilliant career as a playwright could also be quoted as illustrating the new profitability of writing for the theatre: he is reputed to have earned £7000 from the initial success of *Lady Windermere's Fan,* compared with £200 from the serial rights of *The Picture of Dorian Gray.*[31] It may be noted that the American Copyright Act became effective between the appearance of the two works.

Although unproven as a playwright in his own country, Wilde was by no means ignorant of the theatre. His romantic drama, *Vera or the Nihilists,* had in fact been announced for production at the Adelphi in December 1881, but withdrawn, and both this play and his *Duchess of Padua* were staged in New York, however briefly. The wildly improbable plot and inflated style of *Vera* cannot wholly conceal the author's dramatic insight:

(*Goes to the back of the stage, draws aside a curtain. View of Moscow by moonlight*)

has the true Adelphi showmanship, and a recent study[32] points out the precedent established in this play by the epigrammatic Prince Paul Maraloffski, some of his bonnes-bouches being thriftily served up in *Lady Windermere's Fan,* including 'Experience — the name men give to their mistakes'. Wilde's own mistake in *The Duchess of Padua* was to follow the Romantic poets' lead in seeking inspiration from the Elizabethans for a theatre and audience conditioned by wholly changed circumstances, and his experience in seeing the play turned down by Mary Anderson and a failure when staged by Lawrence Barrett led him to a different approach in *Salomé,* which, whatever its extravagances, was entirely a product of the 1890s. Even the apparent affectation of writing it in French made sense, Sarah Bernhardt's attempt to produce it in London being defeated by the censor.

Though an unsuccessful playwright, Wilde's connections with the theatre remained close. He zealously attended the Lyceum, his reactions being characteristically expressed in sonnet form. Thus of Irving in *The Corsican Brothers:*

> These things are well enough — but thou wert made
> For more august creation!

and of Ellen Terry in *The Merchant of Venice*:

> O Portia! take my heart: it is thy due:
> I think I will not quarrel with the bond.

Further, the attention of the London public was regularly drawn in the 1880s and early 1890s to this highly theatrical figure, not merely by *Patience* but through the impersonations of Tree as Scott Ramsey in *Where's the Cat?* and Lambert Streyke in *The Colonel*, of Charles Hawtrey as the Poet in *The Poet and the Puppets*, and of Charles Brookfield as Bertie Twyford in *To-Day*. Wilde's own platform performances, both in America and at home, were undoubtedly valuable training for the role of entertaining an audience in the theatre.

What now seems to many a misalliance between strong drama and lightly turned epigram in Wilde's three serious plays did not worry him, and is usually taken to indicate that he did not view them seriously. Some of his audience did not take them seriously either, as Shaw's comment on *An Ideal Husband* (1895) suggests:

> In a certain sense Mr Wilde is to me our only thorough playwright.
> He plays with everything: with wit, with philosophy, with drama,
> with actors and audience, with the whole theatre.

though Shaw did not underrate Wilde's work on that account, pointing out:

> As far as I can ascertain, I am the only person in London who can-
> not sit down and write an Oscar Wilde play at will. The fact that his
> plays, though apparently lucrative, remain unique under these cir-
> cumstances, says much for the self-denial of our scribes.[33]

In any case not only the wit but the strong drama and the strong sentiments had their admirers. William Archer, a dedicated champion of intellectual drama, remembered twenty years after the first night of *Lady Windermere's Fan* that following the scene in which the lady, having threatened to strike Mrs Erlynne with the fan if she crosses her threshold, instructs her butler to pronounce the guests' names distinctly:

> For my own part, I can aver that, when the curtain fell on the first act, a five-pound note would not have bribed me to leave the theatre without assisting at Lady Windermere's reception in the second act.[34]

Perhaps the key-play in this issue is *A Woman of No Importance* (1893). It has failed to hold the affections of the playgoer or a regular place in the modern repertoire. It is the worst-proportioned of the three plays: the first act has, at Wilde's express desire, 'absolutely no action at all' (and hence was in his view 'a perfect act');[35] the last has absolutely no humour at all, perhaps unintentionally. The moral is spelt out even more slowly than in the others, and not made more palatable by coming from a young American:

> HESTER: . . . You rich people in England, you don't know how you are living. How could you know? You shut out from your society the gentle and the good. You laugh at the simple and the pure. Living, as you all do, on others and by them, you sneer at self-sacrifice, and if you throw bread to the poor, it is merely to keep them quiet for a season.

Yet *A Woman of No Importance* was no less successful than its predecessor; indeed the climactic line: 'Stop, Gerald, stop! He is your own father!' was displayed on every horse-drawn tram in London. Wilde's friend and fellow-Irishman, Vincent O'Sullivan, asserted: 'It was just the coarse strain in Wilde which made the popularity of his plays. He was sentimental in his dramas — not aristocratic',[36] a comment which must refer to the popularity of his plays in the popular parts of the theatre.

On the other hand, their function as problem plays has been greatly overrated. Shaw singled out *An Ideal Husband* for its 'modern note . . . struck in Sir Robert Chiltern's assertion of the individuality and courage of his wrongdoing as against the mechanical idealism of his stupidly good wife',[37] (a decidedly Ibsenite interpretation of swindling the stockmarket), and later dismissed *The Importance of Being Earnest* because 'unless comedy touches me as well as amuses me, it leaves me with a sense of having wasted my evening'.[38] Recently *An Ideal Husband* has been construed as a piece of hidden autobiography: Chiltern's secret representing Wilde's secret (or at least overlooked) bisexuality.[39] But such a view runs contrary to Wilde's whole attitude to the theatre: not merely his contempt for the first-night audience (which may have been forced on him by his aesthetic assumptions) but his amused tolerance of actor-managerial egotism. Thus he told Lewis Waller, who took over Lord Illingworth and created Chiltern: 'Between ourselves I long to see you as Milton's Samson Agonistes', and confided to Alexander and Allan Aynesworth, his Jack and Algy, 'You are neither of you my favourite actor'.[40] He would scarcely trust his secrets to them or their public.

Their stage-history confirms that the plays are comedies, not *théâtre utile*, and as such widely welcomed by audiences long dismissive of profligates and fallen angels. Wilde's women with pasts (including Miss Prism) are mostly delightful company, not melancholy Magdalens. Mrs Erlynne is indeed 'a very clever woman', created by a very clever playwright; Mrs Cheveley's 'face is illumined with evil triumph; there is joy in her eyes' and joy in the eyes of her beholders. Mrs Arbuthnot admittedly seems something of a sister to Mrs Gummidge, but her gloom is at least challenged by Mrs Allonby, another clever woman, who has to be excluded from the play's final moments for that reason. His raisonneurs and dowagers are no less entertaining, but this was predictable. An amusing femme fatale was an innovation. Its author described *Lady Windermere's Fan* to Alexander as 'one of those modern drawing-room plays with pink lampshades',[41] not one of those modern problem plays with social implications. Like many of his comments, it cut more deeply and widely than appeared.

When Wilde decided to spend the summer of 1894 writing the play that became *The Importance of Being Earnest,* he offered it with typical legerdemain almost simultaneously to Alexander, Wyndham, and Hawtrey, partly because he was looking for an immediate advance, but also because he thought it too lightweight for the St James's. His emphasis on the farcical ideas and incidents it contained may have been mistaken or disingenuous, but he was certainly justified in distinguishing it from its predecessors. The suggestion

'Ask him what the origin of his fortune is!'
Scene from Act II of the 1895 Haymarket production of Oscar Wilde's *An Ideal Husband*, showing Lewis Waller as Sir Robert Chiltern, Florence West (Mrs Lewis Waller) as Mrs Cheveley, and Julia Neilson as Lady Chiltern. Sketch by Raymond Potter.

that it was originally set 'in the period of Sheridan'[42] may or may not have substance; its affinities with Gilbert, noted in his review by Shaw and developed in detail with respect to *Engaged* by modern critics, help to define its singularity. Though setting and characters seem shared with the earlier plays, it uses this material to sustain a fantasy of words and conceits, starting with the title itself. Melodrama and sentiment are banished or parodied (as in the 'killing off' of the prodigal brother, the use of aliases in Bunburying, the assumption that because the infant John Worthing was found in Miss Prism's handbag, he must be her illegitimate child), producing a consistent display of comic bravura, free from the bitterness and inflexibility of Gilbert or the sententiousness of Wilde's contemporaries and of his own earlier plays.

It is also much tighter-knit than its predecessors, with a smaller cast and in the original design only two sets, everything after Act I taking place in the garden.[43] One of the most valuable results of this concentration is that the epigrams acquire added humour by coming from characters central to the story, rather than from raisonneurs, passing grandes dames, or even mouthpieces introduced to be witty and then discarded (the Countess of Basildon and Mrs Marchmont in *An Ideal Husband*). A comparison between Lady Bracknell and her fellows suggests that Lady Bracknell is memorable because her pronouncements relate to the characters in the play, not to 'Society' or 'the best people' in general. It is this tautness and timelessness which have established *The Importance of Being Earnest* as one of the most widely popular English comedies outside Shakespeare. The social background is at once relevant and immaterial; relevant to the direction and playing, immaterial to the enjoyment of a capable performance. When Wilde emerged from Reading Gaol he struggled to complete a number of theatrical commissions but abandoned them all, claiming that 'I cannot see myself writing comedy. I suppose it is all in me somewhere, but I don't seem to feel it',[44] and 'It is difficult for *me* to laugh at life, as I used to'.[45] Of course his imprisonment and failing health were largely responsible for this attitude, but there may be a further reason. With his critic's eye he recognised the completeness of *The Importance of Being Earnest*.

The popularity of Wilde's plays in the modern repertoire and the historical interest of Jones and Pinero have obscured the reputations of several dramatists in their vein who pleased both actor-managers and audiences but whose work did not survive their own period. Of these, R.C. Carton was early associated with Alexander at the St James's and Charles Haddon Chambers with Tree at the Haymarket. Carton, like Pinero, turned from acting to writing, and supplied Alexander with pieces in various styles, including a neo-Robertsonian comedy, *Liberty Hall* (1892), and a sub-Pinero problem play, *The Tree of Knowledge* (1897), with an Eve whose present is just as lurid as her past. Carton's later work was closely linked to that of his wife, the formidable Miss Compton, in a series of lightweight comedies, the tone of which is sufficiently indicated by titles such as *Lord and Lady Algy* (1898) and *Lady Huntworth's Experiment* (1900).

Haddon Chambers, an Australian, made himself known through the adventures of his *Captain Swift* (1888), also an Australian, which encompass bush-ranging, illegitimacy, unrequited love and suicide in South Kensington. He also wrote for Tree a second *Mrs Tanqueray* in *John-a-Dreams* (1894), with Mrs Patrick Campbell as another demi-mondaine, this time a professional singer with two lovers, one a poet and honourable if drug-addicted (Tree), the other a baronet but dishonourable. Much more original was the piece Chambers supplied to Wyndham, *The Tyranny of Tears* (1899), a miniature with effectively only five parts in an age of sprawling casts, looking forward to the relaxed comedies of Hubert Henry Davies and even to the delicacy of A.A. Milne or John Van Druten.

None of the playwrights in this group was performed by Irving (though some of Pinero's earliest and shortest plays were staged by him), but Irving did encourage J.M. Barrie to write — on the grounds that 'you have a remarkable way of getting your characters off'[46] — for others, notably J.L. Toole, including the burlesque *Ibsen's Ghost* (1891) and a farce, *Walker, London* (1892). As a hard-working journalist Barrie was prepared to try his hand at most theatrical lines, including comic opera (*Jane Annie; or The Good Conduct Prize*, which D'Oyly Carte put on at the Savoy in 1893, but which won no prizes) and a problem play, *The Wedding Guest* (1900), complete with unmarried mother and nameless child. More in character were the mixture of sentiment and Scots humour Barrie brought to the adaptation of his novel, *The Little Minister* (1897), and the period 'char-r-rm' of *Quality Street* (1902), but it was in the same year that he first displayed the dexterity of stagecraft and blinkered view of human behaviour which were his strength and

125

weakness, with *The Admirable Crichton*. Two years later he contrived to find ways to fly in the fantasy (variously interpreted) of *Peter Pan*, although his biggest success came after his mentor's death with *What Every Woman Knows* (1908). Now the secrets of Barrie's private world are known, the magic he conjured up onstage and the mystery he wrapped around himself offstage have been mercilessly dissected. The substance of his contribution to the early-twentieth-century theatre cannot be similarly explained away.

In stressing the importance for the playwrights of the 1890s of the 'parishioners' of the St James's and other places of theatrical worship, there is a danger of equating the late-Victorian audience with the Restoration: a côterie of titled sophisticates dictating dramatic terms to authors and actors alike. The increased sophistication of those sections of Pinero's or Wilde's public sitting in the stalls was certainly a decisive factor in distinguishing the drama of the 1880s from that of the 1890s. There were, however, other parts of the house. The abolition of the pit at the Haymarket still left the upper circle (or 'family circle') and gallery for the traditional patrons of the Victorian theatre, and it was for them that the playwrights shaped their strong tableaux, or provided broad comedy, particularly as the afterpiece had disappeared and the curtain-raiser was disappearing. As has been suggested, Wilde's plays succeeded at the box-office because of, not despite, their drama and sentiment.

The late-Victorian audience was still cross-sectional. The prices of admission to the Criterion in 1900 confirm this:

> Stalls, 10/6; Dress Circle, 7/—; back row (bonnets allowed), 4/—;
> Family Circle, 4/—; pit, 2/6; gallery, 1/—.[47]

If a small, select house like the Criterion offered a range of prices from 10/6 to 1/—, such vast expanses as Irving's Lyceum or Her Majesty's under Tree had to fill their many cheap seats, and neither Ibsen nor Zola, Henry James nor Shaw could achieve this object. What characterised the West End theatre applied much more strongly to the suburban and provincial scene. The leading actor-managers toured extensively, but the enormous growth of the touring theatre opened up stages for now forgotten companies, sometimes playing London's latest favourite, but often last year's, last decade's, or even no one's favourite but the manager's. There was, in any case, a popular drama flourishing alongside and independently of the gospel according to St James in theatres such as Drury Lane or the Adelphi, which also had its suburban and provincial following. Much of the theatrical world of the 1890s was new and stimulating; much more was old and comforting. It is from these traditional airs that a further selection must be drawn.

NOTES

1  Simon Nowell-Smith (Editor), *Edwardian England 1901–1914* (1964), p. 383.
2  *Theatre*, Vol. 19 (1 April 1892), p. 240.
3  Ibid., p. 242.
4  A.B. Walkley, *Drama and Life* (1907). Reprinted in *Victorian Dramatic Criticism*, ed. George Rowell (1971), p. 255.
5  See George Rowell, 'Tree's Shakespeare Festivals 1905–1913' in *Theatre Notebook* XXIX: 2 (1975).
6  G.B. Shaw, *Our Theatres in the Nineties*, III (1932), p. 206.
7  Johnston Forbes-Robertson, *A Player under Three Reigns* (1925), p. 288.
8  Max Beerbohm, *Saturday Review* (24 February 1900). Reprinted in *Victorian Dramatic Criticism*, p. 145.
9  See Michael R. Booth, 'Public taste, the playwright and the law' in *The Revels History of Drama in English* edited by Clifford Leech and T.W. Craik, VI (1975), p. 53.
10  A.W. Pinero, *The Times*, p. viii.
11  H.A. Jones, *Saints and Sinners*, p. vi.
12  William Archer, *Real Conversations* (1904), p. 21.
13  Walter Lazenby, *Arthur Wing Pinero* (1972), p. 86.
14  Doris Arthur Jones, *Life and Letters of Henry Arthur Jones* (1930), p. 108.
15  G.B. Shaw, preface to *Three Plays for Puritans*, pp. 12-13.
16  *Our Theatres in the Nineties*, I, p. 65.
17  *Play-Making* (1912), p. 94.
18  William Archer, *The Old Drama and the New* (1923), p. 310.
19  Clayton Hamilton, *The Social Plays of Arthur Wing Pinero* (1917), I, p. 12.
20  Reprinted in R.A. Cordell, *Henry Arthur Jones and the Modern Drama* (1932), pp. 155-56.
21  H.A. Jones, 'The Theatre and the Mob'. Reprinted in *The Renascence of the English Drama* (1895), p. 24.
22  *The Renascence of the English Drama*, p. xi.
23  p. 24; Reprinted in Cordell, *Henry Arthur Jones*, p. 208.
24  Doris Arthur Jones, *Life and Letters*, pp. 62-63.
25  Cordell, *Henry Arthur Jones*, p. 82.
26  *The Old Drama and the New*, p. 297.
27  *Michael and His Lost Angel* (1896), p. xv.

28  *Saints and Sinners* (1891), p. xxiv.
29  Doris Arthur Jones, *Life and Letters,* pp. 164-65.
30  Cordell, *Henry Arthur Jones,* p. 216.
31  H. Montgomery Hyde, *Oscar Wilde* (1976), pp. 117, 138.
32  Alan Bird, *The Plays of Oscar Wilde* (1977), p. 23.
33  *Our Theatres in the Nineties,* I, p. 9.
34  William Archer, *Play-Making* (1912), p. 137.
35  H. Montgomery Hyde, *Oscar Wilde,* p. 159.
36  Vincent O'Sullivan, *Aspects of Wilde* (1936), p. 204.
37  *Our Theatres in the Nineties,* I, pp. 10-11.
38  Ibid., p. 42.
39  For example by Rodney Shewan, *Oscar Wilde: Art and Egotism* (1977), p. 178.
40  H. Montgomery Hyde, *Oscar Wilde,* p. 175.
41  Bird, *The Plays of Oscar Wilde,* p. 93.
42  Hesketh Pearson, *The Life of Oscar Wilde* (1946), p. 252.
43  Bird, *The Plays of Oscar Wilde,* p. 170.
44  Rupert Hart-Davies (Editor), *The Letters of Oscar Wilde* (1962), p. 659.
45  Ibid., p. 799.
46  Laurence Irving, *Henry Irving: The Actor and His World* (1951), p. 565.
47  Reprinted in J.C. Trewin, *The Edwardian Theatre* (1976), p. 9.

CHAPTER SIX

# *Traditional Airs*

On the night that *The Bells* opened at the Lyceum there were according to the *Era*,[1] the weekly record of the British stage, seventy-six theatres in the provinces offering legitimate drama (including opera within that category). According to the same source, there were also 170 places of entertainment housing some sort of performance other than drama during that week. These figures call for caution: the total of legitimate performances was certainly greater, since the *Era*, which was also the organ of the licensed victualling trade, reflected entertainment at licensed premises more accurately than at the outposts of acting, such as strolling players appearing in halls that made no claim to be theatres. On the other hand, the *Era Almanack* for 1868 listed three hundred music-halls throughout the country, not all of them active every night or even every week of the year. It seems reasonable to accept the proportion here recorded between legitimate and illegitimate entertainment as accurate enough, though the totals of both kinds were undoubtedly higher.

The range of illegitimate performance was enormous, stretching from full-scale circus and elaborate concert, through mixed bills of every possible description, to solo appearances and even lectures. The non-theatrical activities covered by the *Era* catered for every kind of taste, from those for whom plays and acting were unfathomably intellectual to those for whom the theatre was anathema, or at any rate only tolerable in some conscience-salving disguise. In the latter category three of the items listed are particularly revealing: at the Derby Corn Exchange Mrs Scott-Siddons (a descendant of the majestic Sarah) gave her readings from Shakespeare — 'the entertainment was a rich treat, and it is to be regretted that the audience was so small'. Nearby, at the St George's Hall, Burton-on-Trent, George Grossmith (father of the future D'Oyly Carte star) was more fortunate: his comments 'On the Comic Side of Life' were given 'to a large and respectable audience'. At the Assembly Rooms, Weston-super-Mare, Miss Emma Stanley proved an attraction, even out of season, in her recital 'The Seven Ages of Woman'. These three examples of performances for a public which had renounced theatre-going set the scene for the transformation of the next thirty years.

An examination of the *Era*'s reports from the theatres themselves is notable first for the comparatively small numbers (subject to correction, as has been suggested), and secondly for the division of the companies listed into stock and touring. The stock or resident company was a product of the late Georgian practice of granting to certain Theatres Royal in important towns a patent, protecting them from legal interference and suppression, and thus it was possible to engage a resident company for a season, albeit of greatly varying length. The Industrial Revolution fostered the building in manufacturing towns of theatres equipped to stage the new spectacular drama, and the recruitment of further stock companies, so that the first thirty years of Victoria's reign are often regarded as the peak — quantitatively — of this form of theatrical management; qualitatively they told a different story.

The turning-point is usually cited as 1867, the year the Bancrofts sent out a company from the Prince of Wales's to tour *Caste* with 'full London production', including scenery and costumes. The choice of Robertson's play was significant: his muted effects, calling for reserved force in the actors, were largely beyond the simple lines of business of stock companies offering as many as a dozen different plays in one week. Equally significant was the development during the 1850s and 1860s of a comprehensive, swift, and reliable railway-network throughout the country. London productions of whatever play could not have been toured by horse-and-carriage, or more likely, horse-and-cart. The example of the *Caste* company was soon followed: Irving himself had toured with the St James's Theatre Company in the autumn of 1867, and with *Two Roses* immediately before going to the Lyceum.

What the columns of the *Era* for 26 November 1871 reveal is that the example of the *Caste* company was followed but as yet not widely. Of the seventy-six theatres listed as open that week, sixty-four were occupied by stock companies, and only twelve by touring companies. Three of these presented opera or operetta; the remaining nine included a handful of 'first-class attractions': Mrs John Wood and the St James's Company in burlesque; Charles Young and company in a Robertsonian repertory; Charles Dillon, a favourite tragedian, with his ensemble; the young but promising Wilson Barrett, with his wife, Caroline Heath, and support. Others could not be so classified: Mlle Beatrice in *Frou-Frou*; the 'Little Nelly' Company. The remaining sixty-four theatres filled their stages with more or less familiar faces.

This arrangement, however, was subject to an important modification in the form of the guest appearance, as had been the case throughout the century, and even earlier. Amongst the celebrated names gracing stock companies in the week in question were Dion Boucicault and his wife, Agnes Robertson, appropriately at Dublin; another Irishman in a contrasted style, the tragedian Barry Sullivan, at Liverpool; the favourite farçeur, J.L. Toole, at Hanley; and most surprisingly, at Manchester, a name from another age: Helen Faucit, once Macready's leading lady, long since become Lady Martin. She was fifty-four and played Juliet, Rosalind, and Pauline in *The Lady of Lyons*, as well as Portia and Lady Macbeth, in what were announced as her farewell performances, though she was later to change her mind.

What the railway age had undoubtedly accomplished in the provincial theatre was a major realignment of these guest appearances. Stars like Edmund and Charles Kean, Charles Kemble and his daughter, Fanny, and Macready, had undertaken long tours, quitting London for months and even years, as the means of transport available to them dictated. The network of railways available to a performer in November 1871 allowed much briefer visits. Two of Irving's leading ladies, not needed for *The Bells*, thus appeared on the night of his triumph at Birmingham and Brighton respectively.

Isabel Bateman was playing Fanchette, the part with which she had opened the Lyceum season; her sister, Kate, was undertaking a round of 'heavy' roles at Brighton. Nevertheless the overall picture of entertainment in the provinces is heavily weighted, first in favour of extra-theatrical activity to suit a diversity of tastes, and secondly in the theatres themselves of resident companies, widely graced by visiting names.

To turn from the *Era* of November 1871 to its record of events exactly thirty years later is to witness a transformation scene. On 25 November 1901, Irving was playing not at the Lyceum but at the Chestnut Street Opera House, Philadelphia. The failure earlier in the year of *Coriolanus*, his last production at the Lyceum, had driven him on another American tour, and the Syndicate had let the theatre to William Gillette, making the Atlantic crossing in the opposite direction, for *Sherlock Holmes*. The columns of the *Era*[2] provide an even greater contrast in their account of the provincial theatre. It now conveniently includes a feature 'On the Road' which lists 143 touring productions for the week in question. Nowhere is there a reference to a stock company, and while there were certainly a few to be found, their absence from the pages of the professional organ is a sad comment on their status.

The statistics of this feature make impressive reading. It includes several well-known actor-managers, led by George Alexander and the St James's Company, and also (in no special order) Edward Terry, the Compton Comedy Company, Martin Harvey, Ben Greet, and F.R. Benson. All these were touring with their own groups. Even more striking is the roll-call of musical companies: three with *The Belle of New York* (North, South, Wood's); three with *Floradora*; and three D'Oyly Carte Companies (C, D, and E, their seniors having been suspended). A rather ominous note is struck by their repertory, D and E offering only *The Emerald Isle* (Sullivan's last score, completed by Edward German), and even C having to eke out its traditional Gilbert and Sullivan programme with *The Rose of Persia* (libretto by Basil Hood).

The record of legitimate drama is no less arresting. Amongst several duplications there appear three companies in *The Sign of the Cross*, two in *The Second-in-Command*, and two in *The Silver King* (a title nineteen years old). Admittedly the last-named is competing with two companies offering *Mrs Dane's Defence*, Jones's latest success, but his 'Renascence of English Drama' does not seem to have reached very far into the provinces. The longevity of some of the productions suggests to a modern eye the indestructibility of *The Mousetrap*. *Les Cloches de Corneville* claims to be on its twentieth year of touring — 'Operas may come and Operas may go, but *Les Cloches de Corneville* goes on for ever' boasts its management, and audiences must have concurred a little wearily. Mrs Bandmann-Palmer, a serious actress of undoubted if unsung ability, was on her 'Thirteenth Year of Tour with Company', and *Facing the Music*, 'the best farcical comedy on tour', was in its fifty-third week of No. 1 Tour, a controversial but significant claim. Even so, the extraordinary growth of provincial theatres during the years of Irving's rule in London seems to have created an insatiable demand for attractions. The Princess's Theatre, Hoyland, which claims it is 'now playing to splendid business', is notwithstanding looking for a 'Good Pantomime' to open on 16 December, less than three weeks ahead.

As far as major towns were concerned, the replacement of the stock company brought undoubted benefits. Their audiences could see in Irving and the Lyceum ensemble or the Kendals and their company standards of performance and presentation far above those of the best resident groups thirty years earlier. Not even Shaw would have claimed that his favourite, Barry Sullivan, was adequately supported when playing a round of parts with a company he had met less than twelve hours before the curtain rose. Irving's own acting may have been sub-Sullivan to Shaw, but his ensemble outstripped any stock company's efforts, however gallant.

Nevertheless there were only a handful of Lyceum and St James's companies available, and up to 150 other touring groups. It is against this background of a provincial public fed to a very large extent by factory-produced entertainment that the growing demand for a return to resident companies and even regional drama must be seen. Since this demand first found expression at Manchester six years later, it may be relevant to examine the Manchester bills in greater detail. There are now six theatres (compared with three thirty years earlier), the two leading houses being still the Theatre Royal ('this week the Moody-Manners Opera Company') and the Prince's (with *The Messenger Boy*, 'direct from the Gaiety Theatre, London'). In 1871 their attractions had been respectively Helen Faucit as a guest star and the resident Calvert Company, almost certainly the leading Shakespearean ensemble outside London. But it is further down the street that the situation in 1901 really discourages: of four touring companies, William Greet's at the Metropole offers *The Lady Slavey*, a seven-year-old 'musical play'; Mis Rosalie Valmer's attraction at the Comedy, *The J.P.; or Gay Boulogne,* suggests a somewhat tarnished gaiety; Miss Ida Villars' Company at the St James's is offering *No Man's Land*, a piece which had penetrated no nearer the West End than the Grand, Islington; and Mr Henry Dundas scoops the pool at the Queen's with *Hearts Are Trumps*, the Drury Lane autumn melodrama of 1899. A serious playgoer in Manchester in 1901, blest with second sight, might have cried aloud: 'Miss Horniman to the rescue!'

The Manchester roll of music-halls (three, compared with four in 1871) reflects the national figures. The *Era Almanack* for 1900 lists 226 such halls, compared with 300 thirty years earlier. This drop in fact conceals a change in the whole character and organisation of such houses. The early-Victorian dichotomy of 'supper rooms' (catering to an entirely male, mostly well-to-do, and often badly-intentioned clientèle) and the 'friendly leads' and 'free-and-easy' gatherings on licensed premises by working-class patrons was replaced in the 1850s and 1860s by self-styled music-halls, both in working-class areas (as with the Canterbury in Westminster Bridge Road) and increasingly in central London, with the Middlesex or 'Mo' in Drury Lane and the Oxford in Oxford Street. They remained mostly masculine preserves, and their comedians chiefly male, though female singers and dancers were acceptable, and female patrons if accompanied. The consumption of liquor still constituted an important part of the proceedings. The effect on theatregoing of this development, if negative, was nonetheless beneficial: the rowdier elements who had made themselves heard in the early-Victorian theatre were now more likely to join in the chorus at the Canterbury or Oxford Music-Hall, leaving theatres like the Lyceum free to achieve unique artistic standards.

But a further development in the 1870s and 1880s changed theatregoing more substantially. This was the emergence of the variety house, often at the heart of theatreland, extravagantly designed and expensively decorated, the tables and chairman swept away, drinking confined to the bars, and a quasi-theatrical performance possible on a fully equipped stage. For the London Pavilion (1885), the Empire (1887), the Tivoli (1890), the Palace (1892), and ultimately the London Hippodrome (1900) and the Coliseum (1904) attracted a genuinely cross-sectional audience, as strongly represented on the female side as the male, with the attractions equally distributed. The great music-hall names of the 1890s (Dan Leno, Little Tich, Marie Lloyd) commanded a bigger, better behaved public than the Vances and Leybournes of the 1870s. Even the flickering flame of ballet, extinguished at the opera-houses, was kept alive during these years by the Alhambra and the Empire. Moreover a great deal of pressure on the licensing authorities was exerted by music-hall proprietors to allow dramatic sketches in their bills, and a great deal of pressure by theatre managers to disallow such usurpation.

Even more remarkable than the building of these pavilions and palaces was the duplication of performances, often by the same performer. Since the acts were brief and frequently specialised, while the halls themselves drew on a particular or local audience, one artiste in London or a really big provincial city could play several houses in the same night. The disappearance of tables and tankards from the auditorium was essential to the twice-nightly formula, and allowed a use of both space and talent which time-and-motion experts of today would warmly commend. A 1906 guide to the halls[3] reads more like Bradshaw's Railway Guide than the *Era*, showing as it does the following timetable for the debonair Whit Cunliffe, specialist in 'girl' songs, such as 'It's a different girl again':

| | | | |
|---|---|---|---|
| Chelsea Palace | 7.10 | & | 9.45 |
| Euston Palace | 7.45 | & | 10.40 |
| Oxford Music Hall | | 8.50 | |

The branch of theatrical performance on which music-hall exerted the greatest influence during these years was undoubtedly pantomime. After the reforms and refinements of this genre which Planché as a writer and Madame Vestris (amongst others) as an entrepreneur exercised during the 1830s and 1840s, the Victorian pantomime continued on its free-and-easy way, and Planché's delicate touch can be recognised more readily in the fairy comedies of Gilbert and ultimately in the Savoy Operas than in the pantomime scripts of E.L. Blanchard or H.J. Byron. At least two trends were increasingly apparent: the cutting-down of the harlequinade (and with it the vestigial traces of Italian commedia in the antics of Harlequin, Clown, and Pantaloon) in favour of an opening which expanded to become the raison d'être of the evening; and the rejection of the huge variety of subjects, with 'Harlequin' invariably present in the alternative title, in favour of a handful of stories, mostly derived from fairy-tales, like *Cinderella, Babes in the Wood, Aladdin,* and *The Sleeping Beauty,* though *Dick Whittington* stoutly proclaimed his English origin.

It should be added that several of these subjects were common to pantomime and burlesque (when that term was imprecisely used to describe a piece not conceived as parody), as shown by the frequency of *Aladdin* or *Babes in the Wood* without a hint of harlequinade on the Gaiety bills. The increase in long runs in the 1860s and 1870s was also an important factor in shaping the pantomime scene, since theatres were loth to drop a successful production in favour of a pantomime at Easter or Christmas, and the result was the abandonment of the Easter offering and the concentration on Christmas pantomime at 'short run' houses. Chief of these was Drury Lane, which under the management of F.B. Chatterton struggled to offset the ruin which Shakespeare spelt and the bankruptcy Lord Byron brought (through a revival of *Manfred*) by its Christmas attraction, mostly written by E.L. Blanchard and featuring the Vokes family, a team of dancers and acrobats who set their seal firmly on Drury Lane pantomime in the 1870s. The cast of *Aladdin* in 1874, for example, begins:

| | |
|---|---|
| ABANAZAR, the African Magician | Mr Frederick Vokes |
| KAZRAC, his slave | Mr Walter Vokes |
| ALADDIN | Miss Victoria Vokes |
| PRINCESS BADROULBADOUR | Miss Rosina Vokes |

and there is a Jessie Vokes as the Genius of the Lamp still to come.

The devaluation of the harlequinade is also reflected in this bill, which lists two Harlequins, two Columbines (and a Harlequina), two Clowns and two Pantaloons — suggesting a divertissement rather than the major contribution to the entertainment which an inspired clown like Grimaldi had made to the Regency pantomime.

Miss Victoria Vokes's assumption of Aladdin's role also indicates the popularity which now attended Madame Vestris' practice in extravaganza of playing the hero en travesti, and the general acceptance in pantomime of the function and term 'principal boy'.

While Drury Lane had become the stronghold of pantomime in the West End, a fact acknowledged by Covent Garden which withdrew from opposition after 1887, there was stiff competition in the suburbs. Certain houses specialised in pantomime, offering a particular flavour derived from both subject and performers. The Conquest family, for example, were prolific in acrobats, and provided at the Grecian, Hoxton, and later at the Surrey a series of original pantomime subjects with a strong emphasis on the grotesque, including *The Demon Dwarf, The Spider Crab, The Grim Goblin, The Fiend of the Fungus Forest,* and *The Rock Fiend,* while at the Britannia, Hoxton, the Lanes (who had intermarried with the Lupinos) maintained for sixty years a dynastic rule firmly based on pantomime, with the harlequinade still a prominent feature of the proceedings. It was at the Britannia that a music-hall favourite, 'the Great G.H. MacDermott', appeared in a pantomime, *The Black Statue; or The Enchanted Pills and the Magic Appletree,* in 1874.

This was a precedent of some importance, particularly for Drury Lane. The accession to control there of the young Augustus Harris in 1879 led to a wholesale revision of its policy and methods, not least in pantomime. The names of the Vokes family disappeared from the bills, and Blanchard's was gradually excluded. Harris's taste in pantomime favoured lavish spectacle, above all in the shape of imposing 'processions', and broad humour, more closely related to the new music-hall than the old burlesque. To achieve this end a steady stream of music-hall performers were recruited, starting with Arthur Roberts in the 1880 pantomime, *Mother Goose.* But it was the pairing in 1893 of the diminutive Dan Leno and the elephantine Herbert Campbell in a *Robinson Crusoe* which also included Marie Lloyd and Little Tich that firmly established music-hall stars as the great attraction of Drury Lane pantomime. Leno and Campbell continued to be the mainstay of the Christmas bill until 1903, surviving the change of control in 1896, when Harris died and his stage-manager, Arthur Collins, took over. The music-hall flavoured not only the humour but also the musical fare. In 1900 *The Sleeping Beauty and the Beast* (of which Collins was part-author), with Leno,

Campbell, and Fred Emney senior in the cast, included versions of two of Albert Chevalier's topical songs, 'Mafekin' Night' and 'Our Restaurons', as well as 'Keep to the Right, Boys', cheek-by-jowl with Mendelssohn's 'Spinning-Wheel Chorus' and a good deal of original music by the conductor, J.M. Glover. This extraordinary but characteristic mélange indicates the width of brow to which pantomime now appealed; for many of Drury Lane's patrons it was their chance to see music-hall favourites without exposing themselves in a music-hall.

The twin pillars which supported Drury Lane under first Harris and then Collins were pantomime and melodrama. There had been something of a melodrama tradition under Chatterton (often picturesquely disguised as an adaptation from Sir Walter Scott[4]), but Harris at once seized on the notion of an 'autumn melodrama' as a standard feature, and displayed his confidence in the plan by playing the chief villain (out of seven such) in the first offering, *The World* (1880). From that time until the 1920s melodrama dominated the Drury Lane bills outside the pantomime season. There was still opera during the summer, and the occasional prestige attraction, such as the visit of the Meiningen Company in 1881, which greatly influenced Irving's work, or the appearances of Irving himself more than twenty years later. Melodrama and pantomime, however, ensured Drury Lane's continuity.

Important as spectacle was in any Victorian melodrama, it reached its zenith at Drury Lane at the end of the century and into the next decade. Both Harris and his successor were as much 'play-doctors' as impresarios, though neither would claim the status of playwright. Harris in particular regularly had a hand in the scripts he mounted, taking care to collaborate with experienced writers like Henry Pettitt and Cecil Raleigh. The resources of Drury Lane allowed great emphasis on the visual impact of their work, the effects attempted being an interesting combination of actuality (by reproducing famous places and events) and escapism (by focussing on remote lands and natural wonders — the geographical equivalent of the pantomime pageantry offered at Christmas). Most of the early melodramas Harris presented used a framework of London life and monuments on which to hang a sensational story, often turning on some recent campaign in a remote corner of the Empire. Thus the Zulu War figured in *Youth* (1881), the Sudan campaign in *Human Nature*

(1885), the Burmese in *A Life of Pleasure* (1893), the Matabele Rising in *Cheer, Boys, Cheer* (1895), and the Boer War in *The Best of Friends* (1902). Sensation, however, was not allowed to crowd out sentiment, particularly patriotic sentiment. The climax of the African episode in *Cheer, Boys, Cheer*, presents two tableaux depicting 'A Ravine' somewhere 'On the Road to Fort Salisbury'. In the first, 'The Last Stand', a detachment of British troopers, ambushed by the Matabele, sing 'God Save the Queen' as they are picked off one by one. Finally the hero and his rival are left, both wounded, the latter fatally:

(*Chepstow is left standing alone – he fires a last shot, flings his gun from him, and stands a moment swaying to and fro*)

CHEPSTOW: It's over! We've – done – our – duty. (*Falls*)

(*Loud 'Hurrah' off – scattered Matabele rush in from R. A charge of Cavalry sweeps across the stage.* 'God Save the Queen' *fortissimo from the orchestra*)

In the second tableau, 'Till Death Us Do Part', the dying Chepstow (a Marquis) with the aid of a convenient missionary insists on marrying the heroine, passing by on a trek but treacherously abandoned by the Boer guides. Thus he redeems their engagement which he had misguidedly broken, and endows his widow with the means to marry the hero, a mining engineer. The appeal of these heroic struggles against overwhelming odds, spiced by rivalry for the heroine's affections, is closely comparable to the innumerable battles fought by cowboys or Custer's troops against Red Indians in early films.

On the other hand, the more spectacular the scenery, the less spectacular the acting. Drury Lane companies had much to contend with, as the *Illustrated London News* critic, reviewing *The Armada* (an exception to Harris's rule in that it dealt with a 'period' campaign), pointed out in 1888:

In such plays of pageantry and scenic splendour at Drury Lane acting as an art plays a subordinate part. All its subtlety and refinement are lost on a stage peopled with an army of supernumaries and dedicated to a din. It would require lungs of leather to shout louder than the din of carpenters and scene-shifters.[5]

139

Towards the end of the 1880s a change in the tone of Drury Lane melodrama became apparent. Rather than contrast the actuality of its London scenes with the heroism of its battlefields, the stage began to reflect a more fashionable world, with Society functions regularly portrayed, and Society's leaders listed on the playbills. An early manifestation of this was the introduction of racing and racecourses, often featuring a live horse or horses. Goodwood figured as early as 1886 with *A Run of Luck*; the Derby was regularly shown, in *A Million of Money* (1890), *The Derby Winner* (1894), *The Whip* (1909), and *The Hope* (1911). *The Whip* was particularly admired for its railcrash, and for the villainess's comment on the casualties, after the plot to dispose of the favourite in the accident had failed: 'All Third Class passengers. Dreadful things are always happening to those sort of people'. The Grand National was also used in *The Prodigal Daughter* (1892), and Longchamps furnished one of the scenes in *The Sins of Society* (1907).

Often these racing pieces suggest a return to the equestrian drama at Astley's and the Royal Circus earlier in the century. *The Derby Winner*, for example, features a 'String of horses hooded and clothed, with Stable Lads' which 'pass at back of scene behind gauze as if indistinctly seen through the mist', characters driving a pony carriage and riding cobs and a pony, a mounted villainess who 'cuts Desborough savagely with a riding whip, turns her horse sharply, and canters off stage laughing', a scene at Tattersals with the favourite, Clipstone, all but bought from the bankrupt hero by the villain, another in the Paddock at Epsom, with 'Horses led round, Clipstone followed by Backers and Admirers. Saddling bell rings. Jockeys mount' and the Derby itself. This, however, seems to have presented problems which the Circus Ring at Astley's could have solved. As the *Era* reported:

> It was impossible to represent a run for the Derby with the same effectiveness as one for the Grand National, for the simple reason that any body of horses really galloping at finishing speed must infallibly break their necks against the side walls of the theatre.

On the first night, therefore, Augustus Harris came in front and told the audience that 'Clipstone had been a little awkward at starting, but that he could assure them the horse had really been first past the post'.[6]

What clearly emerges from a piece such as *The Derby Winner* are the patriotic principles of the stable-staff, who put their betters to shame. Clipstone's owner, Lord Desborough, has been unwisely involved with the villainess before marrying; Lady Desborough, incensed by her husband dancing with the lady in question at the Regimental Ball, takes the first train to London, rashly accepting the protection of the jealous Major Mostyn. On the other hand, Clipstone's trainer indignantly rejects Mostyn's bribe to nobble the horse:

> AYLMER (*rising*): No! An Englishman and a sportsman don't take 'is revenge out of a poor dumb animal. The 'oss is favourite. All over the country 'undreds and 'undreds 'ave backed 'im because I train 'im, and they say Joe Aylmer's a honest man. And they're right, sir, I am.

Again, Clipstone's jockey, wrongfully dismissed by Desborough, springs back into the saddle when his replacement is found drugged:

> LEIGH: Stop! Dick Hammond — you are going to ride Major Mostyn's horse. You are wearing Major Mostyn's colours. You are going to try your best to win today for Major Mostyn — the man who ruined your sweetheart, Mary Aylmer.
> MOSTYN: It's a lie!
> MARY (*appearing between Leigh and Desborough*): It's true!
> MOSTYN (*to Leigh*): What has this to do with you, sir? Hammond, get on your horse.
> DICK: No! (*Tearing off cap and jacket*) Ride your damned horse yourself. (*Flings colours in Mostyn's face*) My lord, give me your colours. I've won in 'em before, I'll ride straight and honest, and if Clipstone can win, I'll make him!

The star of Astley's, Andrew Ducrow, might have deplored so much dialogue, but he would have endorsed the sentiments.

When to these sporting events were added such events in the Society calendar as riding in Rotten Row, Oxford versus Cambridge at Lords', and the Military Tournament, together with an assortment of levées, banquets, balls, and garden-parties, all regularly portrayed on the stage of Drury Lane, then Harris's and Collins's melodramas might fittingly be described as the illustrated sporting and dramatic news. Drury Lane drama reflected the preoccupation of theatregoers with the smart set no less than Pinero's or Jones's problem plays, though it was aimed at a different public with simpler tastes and another outlook. *Hearts Are Trumps*, for example, combines a fashionable Private View at Burlington House with a time-honoured melodramatic moment. The heroine has been 'exposed' at the Royal Academy's Summer Exhibition by an unscrupulous artist painting her features on another model's undressed figure. Her 'guardian' rebukes the gaping gentry:

> LADY WINIFRED: What has that dear child ever done that you should dream her capable of forgetting her goodness and her modesty and posing for — this! . . . That picture is a blackguardly outrage on a pure girl; there is but one way to treat it — like this!
> (*Lady Winifred snatches scissors from her chatelaine, and slashes picture across, then seizing canvass, tears it down*) . . .
> BURFORD (*coming forward*): Here — What's that? Stop! Lady Winifred Crosby, that picture is my property! By what right do you —
> LADY WINIFRED: What right? By the dearest right that is given to woman by man or God. *I am her mother!*
> (*Dora with a cry, rushes to Lady Winifred who clasps her in her arms.*
> *Picture*)

Later in the same play, a scene onstage at the Frivolity Music-Hall introduces the Biograph showing a brief 'moving picture' in which Burford (a Brewery Baron) is himself exposed as an overdressed cad. Boucicault, who exploited the camera in *The Octoroon* and the telegraph in *The Long Strike*, would have been proud. These sensation scenes were a pointer to the twentieth century, for they made use of such modern devices as an underwater battle in diving suits (*The White Heather*, 1897), a fight to the death in a balloon (*The Great Ruby*, 1898), and in an airship (*Sealed Orders*, 1913). Ultimately the Biograph was to take over the whole world of sensation drama.

After 1890, when Wilson Barrett left the Princess's with its record of popular drama in such successes as *The Lights of London* and *The Silver King*, the other surviving bastion of melodrama in the West End was the Adelphi, a house associated with that form from its beginning (although sometimes in the threadbare state which occasioned the term 'Adelphi guest' to mean a supernumary lacking verisimilitude in his appearance and acting). Madame Celeste and Benjamin Webster were only two exponents who had thrilled the mid-Victorian public with their own brand of Adelphi melodrama. But the acquisition of the Adelphi lease in 1879 by two Swiss-Italian restaurateurs inaugurated a new era in the Adelphi's history. The Gatti brothers were not themselves performers; they saw their new acquisition as much as an extension of their catering interests as a base for theatrical ambition. Nevertheless, they soon formulated a complementary recipe to Drury Lane melodrama. Though spectacle was not lacking, stirring sentiment proved their stock in trade, and unlike the Drury Lane performer, the Adelphi actor was given his head to rouse the men by his athleticism and enchant the women by his looks. The Gattis brought forward various Adelphi idols, including the experienced Charles Warner for *In the Ranks* (1883), but it was William Terriss who, in two terms of leading the company (1885 – 89 and 1894 – 97), gave the expression 'Adelphi melodrama' a new meaning, and by his association with Jessie Millward as leading lady also provided the theatre with the double attraction that the Lyceum possessed in Irving and Ellen Terry or the Criterion in Wyndham and Mary Moore.

Terriss had earlier appeared in Drury Lane melodrama, including the London production of *The Shaughraun,* but before going to the Adelphi he was prominent at the Lyceum, where his manly, straightforward style provided Irving with a perfect foil to his complex and often sinister characterisations. Ellen Terry, who had played opposite Terriss in *Olivia* at the Court before joining the Lyceum Company, described him thus:

> He had unbounded impudence, yet so much charm that no one
> could ever be angry with him. Sometimes he reminded me of a
> butcher-boy flashing past, whistling on the high seat of his cart, or
> of Phaeton driving the chariot of the sun — pretty much the same
> thing, I imagine![7]

Her comparison may explain why he succeeded as Mercutio in Irving's production, but found Romeo (with Mary Anderson as his Juliet) somewhat beyond him. At the Adelphi he was ideally cast as a man of action, often in the services, whose honour was usually impugned but whose bravery was overwhelmingly displayed and credit ultimately restored. Terriss had served briefly at sea, and sailing and swimming were his chief occupations, so 'Breezy Bill' was an apt and affectionate nickname for him. As a sailor in *The Harbour Lights* (1885) he could sustain the climax of Act III which found him and the injured Lina trapped by the tide:

> *A wave dashes up over them*
> DAVID: Ah, God, the end has come. We are lost, Lina. (*Trying to raise her*) Lina, one effort, it is for our lives.
> LINA (*slowly opening her eyes*): Dave, you can climb. Go, and leave me.
> DAVID: No, Lina, not while God spares my reason and my life to battle for us both.
> (*Business worked up. The tide rises − the cliffs sink. Enter Tom and Jack in boat − as David and Lina are swept off the rocks − and saved!*)

Again as Jack Medway, a petty-officer in *The Union Jack* (1888) and William, an able seaman, in a revival of *Black-Ey'd Susan* (1896) he was in his element. Both were gallant heroes who, under grave provocation, struck their superior officers. Both were pardoned and reunited with their loves.

Army uniform also suited him. He played British soldiers in *One of the Best* (1895) and *Boys Together* (1896), and American soldiers in Belasco's *The Girl I Left Behind Me* (1895) and Gillette's *Secret Service* (1897). But he was in no sense a 'chocolate cream soldier', as Ellen Terry insisted:

> When he was 'dressed up' Terriss was spoilt by fine feathers; when he was in rough clothes, he looked a prince.[8]

Perhaps it was this princely bearing that gave conviction to the sensational court-martial scene in *One of the Best,* inspired by the Dreyfus affair. Dudley Keppel, like Dreyfus, is falsely convicted of espionage:

> *The drums begin to roll − as Sergeant Hennessy steps up to him and strips off his collar and cuffs the drums continue to roll; as each additional mark of his rank is removed Keppel's face depicts the agony which his soul is suffering.*

Poster for *One of the Best* by George Edwardes and Seymour Hicks, performed at the Adelphi in 1895 with William Terriss as Dudley Keppel.

until finally

> KEPPEL: Stay! You may take my name, my honour, my life — but
> you cannot take my Victoria Cross!
> SERGEANT HENNESSY: Unfold your arms!
> KEPPEL: No! The cross is mine!
> GENERAL COVENTRY: Quite right, the law allows it!
> KEPPEL (*to Mary*): God bless and guard you, my dear one. Ah!
> They would have taken my Victoria Cross, but it shall be yours.
> Keep it, darling, some day I shall claim it from you!
> MARY: Dudley!
> KEPPEL: One last kiss — goodbye!
> MARY: Goodbye!
> SERGEANT HENNESSY: Fall in!
> KEPPEL: I am ready!
> (*Mary staggers — falls forward; the drums roll, the band crashes out;
> the mob shout, and Keppel rushes up to gates C., turning back and cries*)
> God Save The Queen!

Since Terriss was the raison d'être of the piece, the ill-used
Keppel had ultimately to be vindicated and (unlike the self-
sacrificing Marquis of Chepstow in *Cheer, Boys, Cheer,* at Drury
Lane) claim his true love's hand and heart. A comparison between
melodrama as presented at the Lyceum, Drury Lane, and the
Adelphi, its three chief resorts in the 1890s, is instructive. The
Lyceum, as has been noted, shunned the contemporary scene and
elaborated on the sinister and sardonic vein in which Irving excelled,
against a period background often tinged with the supernatural,
always with an element of mystery. Drury Lane was essentially an
ensemble house; often its heroes were comparatively minor figures,
and the villains numerous and variegated. The overall picture was
what the audience remembered. At the Adelphi the scenery was
impressive but not overwhelming; the play's impact derived from
the athleticism and forthrightness of Terriss's acting, and from
Jessie Millward's quiet appeal opposite him. Their complementary
talents were as effectively deployed as those of Irving and Ellen
Terry, though visually reversed: Terriss was fair, Jessie Millward
dark.

Two plays of roughly the same date — *Hearts are Trumps* (Drury
Lane, 1899) and *Boys Together* (Adelphi, 1896) illustrate the different

Poster depicting the avalanche in *Hearts Are Trumps*
by Cecil Raleigh, performed at Drury Lane in 1899.

emphases the two theatres placed on their melodramas. Both set their climax on an Alpine peak. In the Drury Lane piece (by Cecil Raleigh) it is the heroine who is lured to the mountain-top by a crooked financier who has insured her life, and the rescue-team consists of the hero (a clergyman) and the artist whose remorse after exposing her at the Royal Academy prompts him to self-sacrifice. Having roped himself to her, he slips and cuts the rope to prevent her being dragged down with him, while the clergyman climbs to her aid. But it is an avalanche which proves the real hero of the evening, by carrying off the financier and the scenic honours at the same time.

*Boys Together* (by Haddon Chambers and Comyns Carr, who seem to have taken a leaf from Sherlock Holmes's last casebook) finds hero and villain struggling on the abyss, and sends the resourceful heroine to the rescue:

> FORSYTHE: At last! You shall go to hell alone! (*with an effort to throw him over — Villars by swinging round defeats him.*) No! Then we'll go together! (*wildly*) We were boys together, you know — let's die together! (*with an effort to fling himself over with Villars*)
> VILLARS (*throwing himself back but falling on the edge with Forsythe*): Fool, madman, I had forgiven you.
> FORSYTHE: Too late! I hate you! Come with me! Come with me!
> (*They roll over together; Forsythe, out of sight, screams. Villars's hand is seen clinging to a piece of projecting rock. Ethel, who has rushed back from the pathway at the commencement of the struggle, now enters and runs upstage*)
> ETHEL: Frank! Frank! (*She kneels at the edge of the precipice.*) . . .
> Quick! Take my hand! I will help you!
> VILLARS (*faintly*): No, no! Keep away! I would only drag you over!
> ETHEL: I must save you! I will! I will!

and, with the aid of 'a long hooked stick which is standing against the penthouse', he is saved.

Terriss's character was as simple and straightforward offstage as on. Shaw wrote the part of Dick Dudgeon for him, but the Diabolonian ethics of *The Devil's Disciple* were beyond him; he fell asleep while the author was reading the play, and Shaw stormed out.[9] His two tours of duty at the Adelphi were separated by a return to the Lyceum to play, amongst other parts, Henry II in *Becket* and Henry VIII, two manly monarchs whose lack of subtlety agreed with his own approach. He then rejoined the Adelphi where, on the night of 16 December 1897, as he arrived to play in *Secret Service*, he was stabbed to death by Richard Prince, a small-part actor, formerly in the company, whose insane jealousy had been exacerbated by the calculated malice of W.L. Abingdon, the leading actor who played villain to Terriss's hero.[10] Thus Adelphi melodrama was enacted outside the Adelphi itself, though its ending was tragically different from the theatrical formula to which Terriss had added a colourful chapter.

His last years at the Adelphi coincided with the first appearance, mostly in music-halls, of an invention that was to transform the entertainment world: the moving picture. For some time variety programmes included a short, silent film, usually recording an actual event, alongside their live acts, and the two coexisted happily. But as the film-makers acquired the skills and confidence to tackle full-length stories, it was to melodrama they turned, and many of the most successful silent films drew on the popular English and American repertoire of the previous fifty years. The cinema, even before 1914, presented a serious challenge to the theatre's dependence on melodrama, for spectacle, its greatest asset, could be enormously enhanced on the screen, and actuality, another of its attractions, made a far bigger impression in celluloid than on the stage. Thus melodrama in the theatre found itself increasingly outbid by the film, and after exploiting the stage melodrama, film-makers like D.W. Griffith created original screenplays. In this sense the twentieth-century successor to Drury Lane spectacle was *Birth of a Nation* and its fellows, while the place in the Adelphi public's affections secured by William Terriss and Jessie Millward was taken over by Douglas Fairbanks and Mary Pickford, and their imitators, worshipped by film fans all over the world. Similarly the young English comedian who had played the music-halls in Fred Karno's *Mumming Birds* in the early 1900s was universally known by 1914 as Charlie Chaplin from the Keystone comedies. The popular theatre underwent a revolution; traditional airs had been transposed for new and all-powerful instruments.

Meanwhile the actor-managers' theatre had to face another challenge — from within. It was raised chiefly in support of a Scandinavian whose work was virtually unknown and unperformed in England until he was over sixty. The campaign to introduce him to English audiences was led by an Irishman, a Scotsman, and a Dutchman. In 1889 Ibsen's work made its first authentic appearance on the London stage, with Shaw, Archer, and J.T. Grein foremost in performing the introductions.

NOTES

1  *Era,* 26 November 1871, p. 5.
2  *Era,* 23 November 1901.
3  Cited in R. Mander and J. Mitchenson, *British Music Hall: A Story in Pictures* (revised edition, 1974), p. 50.
4  For example, *Amy Robsart* (1870), *Rebecca* (1871), *The Lady of the Lake* (1872), *Richard Coeur de Lion* (1874), all by Andrew Halliday.
5  *Illustrated London News,* 29 September 1888.
6  *Era,* 22 September 1894, p. 8.
7  Terry, *Memoirs,* p. 112.
8  Ibid.
9  Jessie Millward, *Myself and My Friends* (1923), pp. 117-18.
10  Seymour Hicks, 'The Murder of William Terriss' in *Between Ourselves* (1930), pp. 36-44.

# CHAPTER SEVEN

# *Independent Means*

The relative values of English and European drama in the latter half of the nineteenth century are usually illustrated by underlining the London theatre's dependence on Paris, especially after the apparent revival of native inspiration during the 1860s. A less familiar comparison can be made by noting that Robertson and Ibsen were almost exact contemporaries and that *Caste* and *Peer Gynt* appeared in the same year, 1867, yet it was not until almost twenty years after Robertson's death that Ibsen received an adequate hearing on the English stage. The restricted repertoire of the London theatre cut off the public not only from contemporary Scandinavian drama, including Björnson and Strindberg, as well as Ibsen, but also from the more daring exponents of French and German drama, such as Zola, Brieux, Hauptmann, and Sudermann. Irving, the Bancrofts, and the Kendals, like their audiences, looked no further than Scribe and Sardou, or their imitators.

Where Ibsen and the Scandinavians were concerned, there was of course a considerable barrier of language as well as taste. Without translations neither English players nor the English public could come to grips with this new and formidable influence on the European theatre. One of the few figures in the British camp capable of assessing Ibsen was William Archer, who had spent a substantial part of his childhood in Norway and acquired a working knowledge of the language. By the early 1880s he was familiar with many of Ibsen's plays and had met the author and discussed his work. Yet *English Dramatists of Today* restricts itself to the comment that 'In Scandinavia the highest literature of the past twenty years has taken dramatic form. Ibsen and Björnson are almost as popular in Germany as in their own country',[1] and devotes the greater part of the introduction to a comparison between English and French drama, unflattering to the former, particularly as regards the English public's preference for cheap French farce like *Les Dominos Roses*. '*Divorçons!* has been played with success in Germany, in Denmark, in Italy; for us it is much too lively.'[2] Either *Ghosts* or *A Doll's House* could have been cited as even livelier, but neither is mentioned, doubtless because they would have been meaningless titles to Archer's readers.

Nor was he in haste to rectify the situation. Though Edmund Gosse had published an article on *Peer Gynt* in the *Spectator* ten years before,[3] Ibsen's growing reputation made little impact in England during the 1880s. Archer's own articles, starting with a contribution to the *St James's Magazine* in 1881,[4] provoked only a modicum of interest, and his free adaptation of *Pillars of Society*, produced (as *Quicksands*) for a single matinee in December 1880, then disappeared for a decade. The travesty of *A Doll's House* which Henry Arthur Jones and Henry Herman (working from an English translation of a German version) in 1884 rendered as *Breaking a Butterfly* pleased neither the purist nor the public. Even willing listeners seem to have turned deaf ears to the Ibsen message. Shaw, for example, claimed to have 'known nothing about Ibsen'[5] when collaborating in 1884 – 85 on the abortive project with Archer which was to become *Widowers' Houses*, and although conscripted by Eleanor Marx to take the part of Krogstadt at a private reading of *A Doll's House* in January 1886, could only recall that he had 'chattered and eaten caramels in the back drawing-room (our green-room) whilst Eleanor Marx as Nora brought Helmer to book on the other side of the folding-doors'.[6]

Gradually, however, interest in this patriarchal figure and his vast if inaccessible output spread across the English Channel, greatly enhanced by the appearance from 1890 onwards of an authorised edition of English translations, under Archer's supervision. At the same time the performance of Ibsen's plays gained momentum. Five years after the débacle of *Breaking a Butterfly*, the genuine text made its historic debut at the Novelty Theatre on 7 June 1889, with Janet Achurch as Nora and her husband, Charles Charrington, as Dr Rank, followed by another performance of *Pillars of Society* in July. Reaction to *A Doll's House*, both pro and con, was such that the run was extended from seven to twenty-four performances, and though there was no rush to bring out the complete Ibsen repertory, his name was now controversial enough to merit inclusion in the Fabian Society's lecture programme on 'Socialism in Contemporary Literature'. Volunteers to give the lectures were called for, and as Shaw wrote afterwards: 'Sydney Olivier consented to "take Zola"; I consented to "take Ibsen" '.[7] Out of this lecture, given on 18 July, 1890, there grew *The Quintessence of Ibsenism*.

The period between the Charringtons' *Doll's House* and the outburst of Ibsen productions in the spring of 1891 (*Rosmersholm* was performed on 23 February, *Ghosts* on 13 March, and *Hedda Gabler* on 20 April) brought to a head the demand for a literary or avant-garde theatre widely advocated in enlightened circles during the late 1880s. Although championed by native supporters, such as Archer and the novelist George Moore, the actual spadework was tackled by a Dutchman, J.T. Grein, who had been working in London since 1885. His Independent Theatre Society announced as its object 'to give special performances of plays which have a LITERARY and ARTISTIC, rather than a commercial value'; its status as a society was intended to circumvent the Lord Chamberlain (following the precedent of the Shelley Society which had staged a private performance of *The Cenci* four years earlier), and a further avowed aim was the encouragement of unconventional English dramatists. But the example of both Antoine at the Théâtre Libre in Paris and Otto Brahm at the Freie Bühne in Berlin, as well as the arguments raging around Ibsen's name, pointed inexorably to *Ghosts* as the first production. Accordingly Archer's translation was produced at the Royalty Theatre on Friday 13 March 1891.

The reception of this more or less scratch performance has been more widely quoted than most London first nights before or since. The more sensational verdicts

> . . . this morbid and sickening dissection of corrupt humanity (*Daily Telegraph*)

> The work of a crazy foreigner which is neither fish nor flesh, but is unmistakably foul (*News of the World*)
>
> a putrid drama the details of which cannot appear with any propriety in any column save those of a medical journal (*Observer*)[8]

have repeatedly found their way into stage-histories of the period, placing the occasion on much the same footing as the first night of *The Bells* as a turning-point in the fortunes of the Victorian theatre. Important as the event proved to be, the réclame attached to it has tended to obscure the true function of the Independent Theatre, which was not founded solely to champion the cause of Ibsen in England, and in the course of its seven years' existence, was responsible for only one other Ibsen premiere — *The Wild Duck* in 1894 — and a couple of revivals.

On the other hand, it undoubtedly contributed greatly to the receptive atmosphere already engendered amongst the enlightened by productions such as *A Doll's House* and *Rosmersholm*, and because of the participation in its work of leading performers in the Ibsen programme, such as Janet Achurch, Elizabeth Robins, and Florence Farr, served to bind together their diverse efforts. The prominence of actresses in this programme was natural and appropriate: parts like Nora, Rebecca, Mrs Alving, and Hedda called for outstanding talent and strong nerves. Shaw in particular noted the importance in these enterprises of performers with advanced or unprofessional backgrounds who

> were products of the modern movement for the higher education of women, literate, in touch with advanced thought, and coming by natural predilection on the stage from outside the theatrical class, in contradistinction to the senior generation of inveterately sentimental actresses, schooled in the old fashion if at all, born into their profession, quite out of the political and social movement around them — in short intellectually naive to the last degree. The new school says to the old, You cannot play Ibsen because you are ignoramuses. To which the old school retorts, You cannot play anything because you are amateurs.[9]

Certainly few of the group he describes could be called orthodox;

Elizabeth Robins and Marion Lea were both American; Mrs Theodore Wright (who played Mrs Alving) had little professional experience; Florence Farr was as much singer as actress.

Equally the impact of Ibsen on the London public was greatly beholden to the new generation of dramatic critics. Their elders, led by Clement Scott and Joseph Knight, had been content to record the steady progress in acting, production, and social acceptability which the actor-managers had conferred on the theatre. Now men such as Archer brought their knowledge of Continental masters to show up the shoddiness of the English repertoire; the elegant style and classical education of A.B. Walkley gave his assessments detachment and range; in due course Shaw, in his own words, began 'a siege laid to the theatre of the XIXth Century by an author who had to cut his own way into it at the point of the pen, and throw some of its defenders into the moat'.[10] Alongside these regulars of the dramatic barricades occasionals like George Moore, Henry James, and Grein himself fired off the intermittent volley. The climate of critical opinion in the 1890s was bold and bracing compared with the relaxed 1880s.

But if the Independent Theatre's choice of *Ghosts* for their debut served the cause of Ibsen well, it served their own purpose less happily. Literary or unconventional English plays proved scarce, and the group's dependence on Continental authors of established reputation continued; Zola in fact provided their second offering, *Thérèse Raquin,* and French and Dutch names featured prominently in succeeding bills. Amongst the writers mentioned in early announcements were Hardy, Meredith, and Stevenson, but nothing by these celebrities was forthcoming, and in the end out of twenty-eight titles produced only two English plays of substance were brought forward: *Widowers' Houses* and Moore's *The Strike at Arlingford* (1893). Several of the principles on which the group planned to operate also proved impractical. The advantages of circumventing the Lord Chamberlain through private performances were largely offset by press and police harassment over the staging of *Ghosts,* and no other unlicensed script was attempted, a decision which excluded *Mrs Warren's Profession* from consideration. Insistence on evening performances also ruled out actors already engaged elsewhere, and severely weakened the standards of achievement. One of the participants, both as actor and director, was the novelist Conal O'Riordan, who later admitted:

> To be sure our average standard was not high. Jimmy Welch in
> *Widowers' Houses,* Mrs Theodore Wright in *Ghosts,* and Elizabeth
> Robins in *Alan's Wife* stand out in the memory. Compared with the
> later work of Harley Granville-Barker and others, our productions
> seem like the rough and tumble of charade.[11]

In fact the administration and financial basis of the Society were
always shaky. Grein himself provided the original capital of £80,
there were only 175 members,[12] and later performances were
frequently thrown open to the general public to swell the coffers. Yet
Grein and his associates did not labour in vain. Ten years after its
dissolution Shaw summed up the Independent Theatre accurately
by first calling it 'that forlorn hope' and then adding:

> That forlorn hope, now that the lapse of time has thrown it into its
> true perspective, is seen to have been the most important theatrical
> enterprise of its time.[13]

To have staged *Ghosts* and *The Wild Duck,* to have launched Shaw as
a dramatist with *Widowers' Houses* and *Candida* (produced on tour in
1897 in harness with *A Doll's House*), were achievements enough,
but there were other seeds sown: an outpost in Manchester, for
example, on whose foundations Miss Horniman was to build her
repertory enterprise, and most important of all in the long run, the
ground was prepared for the Stage Society.

This organisation inherited many of the Independent Theatre's
ideals and several of its personnel. Amongst the signatories of its
original manifesto in 1898 were Janet Achurch and her husband, and
Grein himself served on the reading committee with Charlotte
Shaw. To say that the Stage Society profited by the Independent
Theatre's mistakes is to acknowledge the Society's debt to its
predecessor. Of the lessons learnt, the most valuable were stability
and continuity, to such effect that it managed to operate for forty
years, until finally closed by the outbreak of war in 1939. From the
start the membership was large enough to finance productions from
subscriptions alone: beginning with 300 members, it had expanded
to 1194 by 1904, and was to rise to a peak of 1571 by 1910.[14] By giving
performances on Sunday nights and Monday afternoons the Society

could employ actors working in other theatres (a step doubly desirable in view of its flat rate of payment — one guinea per production). By sticking rigidly to its Society status it could and did dispense with the Lord Chamberlain's approval, thereby achieving performances of *Mrs Warren's Profession,* Granville-Barker's *Waste,* Maeterlinck's *Monna Vanna,* and three of Brieux' plays, all of which had been denied a licence. Featured amongst the early programmes were such untried British playwrights as Granville-Barker (*The Marrying of Ann Leete*), St John Hankin (*The Two Mr Wetherbys*), and Somerset Maugham (*A Man of Honour*), whilst European drama was represented by Ibsen, Tolstoy, Hauptmann, Maeterlinck, and Gorki, as well as Gilbert Murray's version of Euripides' *Andromache.*

The Society's very first production, however, was *You Never Can Tell,* at the Royalty (birthplace of the Independent Theatre) on 20 November 1899, and it can confidently be said of these early years that Shaw launched the Society and the Society helped to launch Shaw, since its programmes up to 1905 included *Candida, Mrs Warren's Profession, Captain Brassbound's Conversion, The Admirable Bashville,* and *Man and Superman.* It also did much to launch Granville-Barker, both as actor and director, in addition to staging *Ann Leete.* Without the opportunities offered him by the Society (for example as Marchbanks and Frank Gardner), the invitation to the Court in 1904 and all that followed from it would scarcely have come his way.

Shaw's work is so firmly linked with the declaration of theatrical independence in the 1890s that it is easy to take his contribution for granted. In fact it demands careful distinction between Ibsenite, dramatic critic, and dramatic practitioner. The first of these functions substantially preceded the other two, since *The Quintessence of Ibsenism,* capitalising on the furore which possessed the theatrical press on matters Ibsenite, appeared in October 1891, over three years before its author became critic of the *Saturday Review.* The form of Shaw's contribution to the debate — considerably longer than earlier statements, whether pro or con, but still easily digested in a morning's study — established his reputation in the field. Prejudiced and perverse though much of his treatment of Ibsen's work may seem, it proved a rallying-cry for the dramatist's admirers and a punch-bag for his detractors. Even Irving paid the little-known Shaw a back-handed compliment by announcing in a speech at Liverpool less than a fortnight after the book's publication:

> I have been reading lately a little book, about what is called 'Ibsen-
> ism', and I learn, in the polite language of the writer, that 'our
> finished actors and actresses cannot play Ibsen because they are
> ignoramuses'. I thought that some of our younger actresses had
> played Ibsen rather well, though this, it seems, is because they are
> novices in art but experienced in what is called 'the political and
> social movement' . . .

and continuing in this ironic vein:

> I don't know whether the Ibsen drama will obtain any permanent
> standing on our stage — and if Ibsen drama be excellent drama I
> most certainly hope it will — but it is a comfort to find that in the
> opinion of the author I have quoted Shakespeare will not be entirely
> extinguished by the genius who is to show us that we are 'ignora-
> muses'.[15]

During the lull in productions of Ibsen between *Hedda Gabler* in
April 1891 and *The Masterbuilder* in February 1893 Shaw was also
active in encouraging such devotees as Florence Farr and Elizabeth
Robins, and the performance of *Widowers' Houses* in December 1892
succeeded in keeping Ibsen's name in the papers almost as effectively
as it publicised Shaw himself, since the author was variously
described as 'An ardent admirer of Ibsen's methods' (*Daily
Telegraph*), 'The London Ibsen' (*Sunday Sun*), 'A zealous Ibsenite'
(*Weekly Dispatch*), and 'The high priest of Ibsenism' (*Piccadilly*).[16]

Nevertheless, by the time Shaw took up his post as dramatic critic
of the *Saturday Review* in January 1895, the early and bloodiest
battles of the Ibsen campaign had been fought. Where Ibsen was
concerned, therefore, G.B.S. had perforce to restrict his column to
the comparatively peaceful premieres of *Little Eyolf* (1896) and *John
Gabriel Borkman* (1897), or reassess the significance of earlier plays
when revived, including the performances in French of *Rosmersholm*
and *The Masterbuilder* by Lugné-Poë's Company when they visited
London in 1895, and their Paris production of *Peer Gynt* in 1896.

The full force of Shaw's scorn fell in consequence on the actor-
managers and their repertoire, with its substitution of Mayfair
melodrama for rigorous intellectual exercise, and so-called problem

plays about ladies with lurid pasts and uncertain futures for genuine problem drama, defined as 'the presentation in parable of the conflict between man's will and his environment'.[17] Clearly his vision of the theatre and its function conflicted strongly with that of both managers and audiences. Entertainment was not the whole object of theatregoing; indeed it scarcely entered into G.B.S.'s scheme of things. While noting that Shakespeare offered his audience a comedy called *As You Like It*, and a modern playwright like Barrie was content to follow his lead, Shaw refused

> as a contemporary of Master-Builder Solness to be done out of my allowance of 'salutary self-torture'. People don't go to the theatre to be pleased. There are a hundred cheaper, less troublesome, more effective pleasures than an uncomfortable gallery can offer. . .[18]

Instead he emphasised the function of the theatre as a weekday pulpit, and looking back on his years as a dramatic critic, asserted his belief that 'it is as important as the Church was in the Middle Ages, and much more important than the Church was in London in the years under review'.[19]

Such pronouncements suggest Shaw the critic functioning as his own John the Baptist, and heralding his own coming as the Messiah of the New Drama. Indeed his earliest plays pay lip-service to such an intent. The critical reception of *Widowers' Houses* fell little short of that for *Ghosts* in its sense of outrage — and Shaw compounded his offence by lecturing the first-night audience from the stage. 'Not a play — a pamphlet' was a frequent if restrained comment, and the critic of *The Colonies and India* noted with unintended precision: 'Mr Shaw wishes to utter a tirade against certain abuses; and he thinks the theatre a suitable pulpit for his utterances'.[20] The author's choice of *Unpleasant Plays* for the title of his first collection suggests the 'salutary self-torture' of the critic put into practice, particularly as he defined their technique as 'playing off your laughter at the scandal of the exposure against your shudder at its blackness'.[21]

Yet as the *Plays Pleasant* succeeded their unpleasant predecessors, and after them the *Plays for Puritans*, the balance between laughing and shuddering shifted steadily in favour of the former. Shaw the practitioner knew more than Shaw the preacher was prepared to admit: that sermons must entertain if they aspire to elevate. Indeed

159

even the earliest plays silently acknowledge this necessity. The lasting impression left by *Widowers' Houses* is the outrageously comic transformation of the servile rent-collector, Lickcheese, into fur-coated entrepreneur; *The Philanderer* spends a whole act satirising the pretensions of 'the Ibsen Club'; and *Mrs Warren's Profession,* for all its genuine shock tactics, combines coarseness with comedy in the characters of Sir George Croft, Samuel Gardner, and Mrs Warren herself.

Shaw used his years on the *Saturday Review* to equip himself for the task of transforming 'their' theatre of the 1890s into 'his' theatre of the 1900s. In particular he set himself to rework the fashionable formulas he analysed nightly at first from the gallery, later from his critic's stall. Thus *Mrs Warren's Profession* constituted his play about a woman with a past (prostitution) and present (brothel-keeping) — both careers being worlds removed from the conventional notoriety of Paula Tanqueray or Agnes Ebbsmith. The infatuation of Eugene Marchbanks for Candida Morell has much in common with Jones's handling of this situation in a series of plays, except that the setting is a Hackney parsonage, not a Mayfair drawing-room, and the lady finally rejects her admirer because her husband needs her support, not because she needs his (as in *Rebellious Susan* or *The Liars*).

The same process of reworking is evident in the *Plays for Puritans*, inspired by the costume dramas which dominated the Lyceum and Adelphi stages during these years. *Caesar and Cleopatra* and *The Devil's Disciple* share their subject matter with Shakespeare and Boucicault respectively, but Shaw's Caesar is Cleopatra's tutor, not her lover, and Dick Dudgeon risks his life to demonstrate his Diabolonian principles, not an unrequited passion for Judith Anderson. Shaw did not hesitate to underline his sources, labelling *Arms and the Man* 'an anti-romantic comedy' and boasting that *You Never Can Tell* catered for 'the popular preference for fun, fashionable dresses, a little music, and even an exhibition of eating and drinking by people with an expensive air, attended by an if-possible-comic waiter'.[22]

Unlike most of the 'independent' school, Shaw also designed his early plays for leading players of the day, and though they mostly declined the compliment, their successors had reason to be grateful. Thus the Strange Lady and Lady Cicely Waynflete were made for

Ellen Terry; Caesar and Cleopatra for Forbes-Robertson and Mrs Patrick Campbell; Dick Dudgeon and Judith Anderson for Terriss and Jessie Millward. On one occasion at least the author did not recognise his inspiration until the work was done. Of Charteris in *The Philanderer* he notes: 'I had written a part which nobody but Charles Wyndham could act in a play which was impossible at his theatre',[23] and in a copy of his plays presented to that actor, he added: 'Ah! si Charles Wyndham voulait — ou si les autres pouvaient!'[24]

Shaw's apprenticeship to the theatre of the 1890s prepared him for the more arduous work he tackled as soon as the theatrical time was ripe. That hour struck with the new century and the growing recognition of his powers brought about partly by publishing his early plays, partly by their success in America and on the Continent, but above all by the platform afforded him in the Stage Society's performances. The plays with which he launched the Court Theatre seasons, *John Bull's Other Island* and still more *Man and Superman*, with their disdain of conventional form, their extended debates and far-reaching arguments, marked a new phase both in his own development and in the development of English drama. Henceforward he needed no formulas to rework, and was himself the model that others strove to copy. But whether wooing Ellen Terry with the Sardouesque situations of *The Man of Destiny* or stretching the intelligence and stamina of the Court audience with *Major Barbara* and *The Doctor's Dilemma*, Shaw consistently displayed the mental vigour and verbal attack which still delight his public. The gifts he shared with his fellow-Irishman, Wilde — mastery of language as a theatrical medium and a confident command of stagecraft — go far to explain why their work, though greatly differing in approach and subject-matter, still holds the stage so firmly almost a century later.

If writers like Shaw and organisations like the Independent Theatre and Stage Society represented one kind of theatrical independence, another individual, William Poel, and another organisation, the Elizabethan Stage Society, voiced opposition to the fashionable Shakespeare productions of Irving and his imitators. Encouraged by the claims of contemporary scholars that the study of Elizabethan drama demanded a study of the Elizabethan stage, a movement gathered support to perform Shakespeare on platforms either chosen for their likeness to the theatre of his day (as provided by the Inns of Court or Halls of the Livery Companies) or reconstructed within modern buildings for this purpose. But Shakespeare on Shakespeare's stage was only part of Poel's crusade; an even more cherished cause was Shakespeare spoken as Shakespeare wrote and intended, the second part of this aim being less readily established than the first. To Poel, a remote and austere figure whose enthusiasms were fuelled as much by mysticism as scholarship, the laboured and idiosyncratic delivery of Shakespeare's verse by Irving or Tree represented music without melody; the tones were even more important than the sense, and much of his work took the form of directed readings of poetic drama, including ten years as Instructor of the Shakespeare Reading Society from 1887 to 1897.

For a further ten years from 1895 to 1905 he was able to express his ideas more fully through the activities of the Elizabethan Stage Society, whose productions gained a good deal of attention, favourable and unfavourable, depending on the writer's loyalties. Shaw was one of their strongest supporters, Poel's taste in decor making a welcome contrast from the overcarpentered and upholstered scenes at the Lyceum. One of the earliest of the Society's productions, *The Comedy of Errors* in the Hall of Gray's Inn in December 1895, was hailed by him as 'a delectable entertainment which defies all description by the pen',[25] surely a unique tribute from that particular pen, and subsequent achievements, such as his *Measure for Measure* at Manchester in 1908, were warmly received by another of his admirers, C.E. Montague.

Nor was Poel's work limited to Shakespeare. He explored other Elizabethans, notably Marlowe, re-establishing *Dr Faustus* as an actable play and directing a memorable *Edward II* in 1903, with Granville-Barker in the name-part. Probably the most momentous of his discoveries was *Everyman*, unperformed and virtually unknown in England since the sixteenth century. It was Poel's biggest — indeed his only — popular success, widely toured and regularly revived, although the enormous public it has gained since the performance in the Master's Court of the Charterhouse in July 1901 has not always realised its debt to Poel. Following the financial collapse of the Elizabethan Stage Society in 1905, he found other outlets, notably Miss Horniman's pioneering platform in Manchester, and in the 1920s was closely associated with the Elizabethan Stage Circle.

It is true that for a professed purist his methods were sometimes oddly inconsistent. The texts used were certainly fuller than those of the actor-managers, but often strangely transposed or conflated and just as sternly Bowdlerized. His choice of costume too could be wildly eclectic, causing Archer to describe him as 'a non-scenic Beerbohm Tree',[26] and he maintained an extraordinary preference for casting women in leading male roles, including Everyman. The actress engaged to play Valentine in *Two Gentlemen of Verona* cannot be blamed for her tears when reproached because

> Of all Shakespeare's heroes Valentine is one of the most romantic, one of the most virile. I have chosen you out of all London for this part, but so far you have shown me no virility whatsoever.[27]

Yet Poel's teaching was well heeded and profitably applied — by Lewis Casson, who worked with him, notably at the Manchester Gaiety; by Robert Atkins in his years at the Old Vic; and above all by Granville-Barker in his seasons at the Savoy between 1912 and 1914, from which modern Shakespeare production is often dated.

While Poel was exploring new avenues with the Elizabethan Stage Society, another pioneer was breaking ground at such unlikely locales as the Hampstead Conservatory of Music and the Hall of the Imperial Institute, South Kensington. Gordon Craig, the son of Edward Godwin and Ellen Terry, was born of fine theatrical stock and served a valuable apprenticeship in the Lyceum Company, but the artist in him soon took over from the actor, and after experimenting as a book-illustrator, he struck up a stimulating partnership with the musician, Martin Shaw. Out of their aspirations sprang the Purcell Operatic Society, a group, like the Elizabethan Stage Society, drawn mostly from talented amateurs which in 1900 'rediscovered' *Dido and Aeneas,* and followed this with the 'Masque of Love' from *Dioclesian,* and then Handel's *Acis and Galatea.* Craig's preoccupation with music-drama at this stage may be seen as a revolt against the subjection of the visual to the spoken, whether in the commercial theatre of the actor-managers or the intellectual drama of the avant-garde movement. Music, on the other hand, fully complemented the sensory appeal of his simple but striking designs, which abolished conventional wings and borders, employed unfamiliar materials imaginatively lit (mostly from above and in front, not by the standard footlights and 'ladders' in the wings), and drew on rich, subtle, unified colour schemes, chiefly contrived by the lighting.

As with Poel's recourse to the Inns of Court or Livery Companies, the choice of improvised stages for the Society's work enhanced the originality of Craig's approach. The tiered concert platform of the Hampstead Conservatory, for example, provided an impressive, wholly non-representational setting for *Dido and Aeneas*, while the Hall of the Imperial Institute in which, in 1902, he staged Laurence Housman's *Bethlehem* was swathed in blue cotton drapes, partly to overcome acoustic problems, partly to envelop the audience in appropriate atmosphere. Even when the Purcell Society took over a conventional stage, it was in an unconventional locale, such as the Coronet Theatre in Bayswater where the 'Masque of Love' was first done, or the unfashionable Great Queen Street Theatre, in which *Acis and Galatea* gained considerable réclame and lost a good deal of money.

Nevertheless Craig's growing reputation persuaded his mother to sponsor a season under his direction at the Imperial (also off-centre) in the spring of 1903. His choice of Ibsen's *The Vikings*, with its Wagnerian theme and setting, suggests an extension of the operatic work of the Purcell Society. Again, as with the earlier productions, the theatre itself was substantially modified to accommodate Craig's simple but imposing designs and unorthodox lighting. However, the company, seasoned professionals including Ellen Terry herself instead of malleable amateurs, found it difficult to meet the revolutionary demands of their director, critical and public reaction was polite but puzzled, and the production was soon withdrawn in favour of a hastily concocted revival of *Much Ado about Nothing*. Even here there was originality in Craig's handling of the Cathedral scene, with two columns set against grey drapes and lit from an invisible stained-glass window, surely a conscious reaction against one of the great 'archaeological' achievements in Irving's production of the play. Nevertheless the Imperial season ended abruptly, and with it Craig's career in the English theatre. He was only thirty-one, and lived to be ninety-four, writing, designing (for Continental stages), learning and teaching. In due course the inspiration which the English theatre had declined to foster bore fruit through the work of his pupils and admirers, European and American. The tiny ripples he stirred up in the theatrical pond before 1904 still flow as strong currents in modern scenic practice.

Amongst the audience which applauded *Dido and Aeneas* and the 'Masque of Love' was W.B. Yeats, who claimed that 'they gave me more pleasure than I have met in any theatre these ten years'. Yeats's own connection with the English theatre stretched back almost ten years to the production of his *Land of Heart's Desire* during the season at the Avenue which included *Arms and the Man* and was financed anonymously by Miss Horniman. While Craig was staging his operatic experiments, however, Yeats was more immediately concerned to launch an Irish theatre, and one of the results was the first visit to London of the Irish National Theatre Society, who gave two performances at the unlikely venue of the Queen's Gate Hall, South Kensington, on 2 May 1903, with a programme including *The Hour Glass* and *Cathleen-ni-Houlihan*. They could only play on a Saturday, since they were all still amateurs, and Frank Fay, one of their founding members, recalled:

> Twenty minutes before the curtain rose we got news that one of our principal actresses was too ill to go on, which I need not say filled us with consternation. But one of the other ladies volunteered to play the parts, and Mr Gwynn announced this from the stage. Fortunately, however, the actress who had been taken ill recovered in time to appear, and the evening performance also passed off without a hitch.[28]

Both on this occasion and on a return visit to the Royalty Theatre in March 1904 the London press voiced surprise and delight that music and poetry could be so naturally combined. A.B. Walkley led the chorus:

> First and foremost, there is the pleasure of the ear . . . We had never realised the musical possibilities of our language until we had heard these Irish people speak it.[29]

The consequences for Irish drama of these modest beginnings were momentous. Their effect on English drama was perhaps one of promise rather than performance. The Stage Society, for example, included Yeats's *Where there is Nothing*, produced by Granville-Barker at the Court in June 1904, in one of the programmes which preceded the Vedrenne-Barker management, opening with the *Hippolytus* in Gilbert Murray's translation in October of that year. Poetic drama was undoubtedly planned as an important part of the project, but Shaw and the play of ideas increasingly took over. The *Hippolytus* was followed by *John Bull's Other Island,* written for but rejected by the Irish National Theatre, in which an Englishman succeeds because he is too stupid to recognise defeat, and an Irishman fails because he is too sensitive to risk victory.

The Independent Theatre, the Elizabethan Stage Society, and Craig's early productions all voiced a protest against the established practices of the actor-managers as most conspicuously displayed at the Lyceum, offering alternatives to their repertoire, their presentation of Shakespeare, and the conventional methods by which they set their stage. Like most protests, they demonstrated that opposition is rarely self-sufficient, that originality cannot sustain itself without forethought and planning, and that even the most inspired enterprises demand private patronage or public support if they are to succeed. Nevertheless, each made a sufficiently strong impression to secure disciples who carried on where their leaders were forced to break off. All three experiments can fairly be said to have prepared the way in the 1890s for important features of the twentieth-century stage.

## NOTES

1  William Archer, *English Dramatists of Today,* p. 6.
2  Ibid., pp. 2-3.
3  *Spectator,* 20 July 1872.
4  William Archer, 'Henrik Ibsen', *St James's Magazine,* January—February 1881.
5  Preface to *Major Barbara* (1907), reprinted in *Prefaces by Bernard Shaw* (1938), p. 115.
6  Preface to *The Irrational Knot* (1905), reprinted in *Prefaces by Bernard Shaw,* p. 689.
7  Preface to *The Quintessence of Ibsenism* (1891), reprinted in *Major Critical Essays* (1932), p. 11.
8  See Michael Orme, *J. T. Grein: The Story of a Pioneer 1862– 1935* (1936), p. 87.
9  Appendix to *The Quintessence of Ibsenism* 1st edition, reprinted in *Shaw and Ibsen* edited by J.L. Wisenthal (1979), pp. 226-27.
10  G.B. Shaw, 'The Author's Apology' in *Our Theatres in the Nineties* (1932), Vol. I, p. v.

11  Foreword to Michael Orme, *J.T. Grein*, p. 16.

12  Orme, *J.T. Grein*, p. 71; N.H.G. Schoonderwoerd, *J.T. Grein: Ambassador of the Theatre 1862–1935* (1962), p. 100.

13  In his obituary of Ibsen originally published in the *Clarion* (1 June 1906) and reprinted in Wisenthal, *Shaw and Ibsen*, p. 240.

14  Mary Jane Watson, 'The Independent Theatre Movement in London 1891–1914' (unpublished M.Litt. thesis, University of Bristol, 1970), p. 82.

15  Speech to the Liverpool Philomathic Society, 14 October 1891, reported in the *Liverpool Daily Post*, 15 October 1891, and reprinted in Wisenthal, *Shaw and Ibsen*, pp. 18-19.

16  See preface to *Widowers' Houses* (1893), reprinted in *Prefaces by Bernard Shaw*, p. 704.

17  Preface to *Mrs Warren's Profession* (1902), reprinted in *Prefaces by Bernard Shaw*, p. 228.

18  Review of *The Little Minister* in the *Saturday Review*, 13 November 1897, reprinted in *Our Theatres in the Nineties*, III, p. 246.

19  'The Author's Apology' in *Our Theatres in the Nineties*, I, p. vi.

20  Preface to *Widowers' Houses*, reprinted in *Prefaces by Bernard Shaw*, p. 707.

21  Ibid., pp. 702-3.

22  Preface to *Plays Pleasant* (1898), reprinted in *Prefaces by Bernard Shaw*, p. 730.

23  Preface to *Plays Unpleasant* (1898), reprinted in *Prefaces by Bernard Shaw*, p. 720.

24  Mary Moore, *Charles Wyndham and Mary Moore* (1925), p. 123.

25  *Saturday Review*, 14 December 1895, reprinted in *Our Theatres in the Nineties*, I, p. 275.

26  *The Nation*, 5 July 1913, reprinted in Robert Speaight, *William Poel and the Elizabethan Revival* (1954), p. 105.

27  Speaight, *William Poel*, p. 121.

28  In *Towards a National Theatre. Dramatic Criticism*, ed. Robert Hogan, Irish Theatre Series 1 (1970), p. 104.

29  *Times Literary Supplement*, 8 May 1903, reprinted in Hugh Hunt, *The Abbey: Ireland's National Theatre 1904–1979* (1979), p. 44.

CHAPTER EIGHT

# *Accolade*

When Irving received his knighthood in 1895, he earned for the actor's profession the Royal recognition which literature (Scott, Tennyson), music (Bishop, Mackenzie, Sullivan), and painting (Leighton, Millais, Burne-Jones), had all enjoyed for many years. As already mentioned, the first approaches had been made twelve years earlier on the eve of the Lyceum Company's departure for America in the summer of 1883. Irving's grounds for refusing the honour on that occasion were professional, not personal. The intermediary employed reported back:

> . . . he would not accept it; he said that an actor differed from other artists, musicians, and the like, in that he had to appear in person every night appealing directly to the public favour . . . that there was a fellowship among actors of a company that would be impaired by any elevation of one member over another; that his strength as a manager and power as an actor lay far more in the suffrages of the plain folk in the pit than in the patronage, however lofty, of great people; that he knew instinctively that large numbers of these same plain folk would be offended at their simple Henry Irving accepting decorations of a titular kind . . .[1]

In advancing such reasons Irving was clearly aware of the jealousy with which he was still regarded in many circles, theatrical and non-theatrical, and was anxious to allay such feelings as far as he could. By 1895 the position was materially changed; not only had he consolidated his claim to the leadership of his profession but public respect for that profession now extended to many of his colleagues and competitors. Irving might still be the chief, but he was by no means unique, and actor-managers like Bancroft (in his retirement), Hare, the Kendals, Wyndham, Alexander, and Tree shared the loyalty and affection towards the theatre and theatre men which characterised the last chapter of Victorian stage-history.

It was a complete coincidence that the gazetting of Irving's honour should be followed two days later by the pronouncement of Oscar Wilde's sentence, but had the actor's achievements been less widely recognised, the dramatist's downfall might easily have cast a ruinous slur on the calling they both served. In the event Irving's knighthood was the subject of universal rejoicing and congratulation, an expression of approval warmly endorsed two years later when Bancroft was similarly honoured during the Diamond Jubilee celebrations. When to these examples are added the honours conferred on the theatrical profession by Edward VII (knighthoods for Wyndham, Hare, and Tree amongst the actors, and for Burnand, Gilbert, and Pinero from the writers), the assimilation of that profession into the established orders is self-evident.

Ten years after he received the accolade from Queen Victoria at Windsor, Irving received his final tribute: a public funeral in Westminster Abbey and interment in Poets' Corner near Garrick's monument. The occasion, stage-managed by George Alexander, most discrete of directors, was graced by representatives of the King, Queen Alexandra, the Prince and Princess of Wales, and leaders from every walk of life. Only one slight setback marred the arrangements; an invitation sent to the former dramatic critic of the *Saturday Review* was declined on the grounds that 'Literature had no place at Irving's graveside'. The shock caused by this contentious statement was immediately aggravated by a sentence in the obituary Shaw wrote for the *Neue Freie Presse* of Vienna, which, mistranslated into German and then back into English, appeared in the British press as: 'He was a narrow-minded egoist, devoid of culture, and living on the dream of his own greatness'. Not surprisingly, the family denounced Shaw as 'a most unmitigated Yahoo', and Ellen

Terry told him roundly: 'I can't understand how one without gross food in him, who takes no wine to befuddle his wits, can have been so indelicate'.[2]

Later he was to put the record straight by affirming: 'Irving had splendidly maintained the social status of the theatre, and greatly raised that of the actor; but he had done nothing for contemporary dramatic literature',[3] a verdict with which few would now be inclined to quarrel. Undoubtedly it was the stability of the English theatre which characterised it in the last three decades of the nineteenth century, and to this stability Irving — effectively the raison d'être of the Lyceum throughout the entire period, and actually its directing force for twenty years — contributed an incalculable amount. The contrast between his record and (say) Macready's or even Bancroft's is total. Though both these men were skilled performers and sensitive directors, their perseverance and sheer stamina seem puny by comparison with Irving's. In an acting career of over forty years Macready managed his own London theatre for no more than six (divided between Covent Garden and Drury Lane). Bancroft admittedly came to management early (by way of marriage to his leading lady), but even he gladly resigned his responsibilities after eighteen years, at the age of forty-four. Irving remained leading man at the Lyceum from his thirty-fourth to his sixty-fifth year, sustaining the double role of star and impresario for all but seven of these years. Nor was his kingdom limited to the playhouse in Wellington Street; increasingly his authority extended throughout the theatrical world, and for over twenty years he could call on the loyalty of the New World's audiences to redress the financial balance of the Old.

With a performer as hypnotic and individual as Irving, it was inevitable that his acting and his image should impress itself on the era to which he gave his name. 'Theatre in the age of Irving' immediately conjures up a vision of one of the famous roles: Mathias, Shylock, Mephistopheles, Becket are only four out of a dozen which might be cited — to conjure up the essential theatrical quality of that period. But the abiding impression left by Irving the actor is powerfully supported by testimony to Irving the impresario. The scale on which he worked; the dedication he gave to that work; the artistry he brought to the visual impact of all his productions; his insistence on the stage as 'another world', illuminated by the magic combination of human insight and theatrical limelight which he commanded — these are the essential features of the Irving era which its theatregoers experienced and its records preserve, however fitfully.

Of course the history of the Lyceum during these thirty years is by no means the whole history of the English theatre at that time. In style and taste he swam against the prevailing currents, a Romantic contending with the naturalist forces in European drama, a Titan fighting against the growing strength of ensemble acting, realistic settings, contemporary themes. The measure of his success was that more than thirty years after his first triumph in the part he could still pack theatres by his performance as Mathias in *The Bells*. The measure of his failure was that he had no choice but to do so. He could not afford to retire, and though he was undoubtedly happy to die in harness, his admirers wished it could be a lighter harness. Not for him the small but rewarding cameo role, but also not for him the challenge of creating a new character in a new drama: the Man of Destiny, John Gabriel Borkman, Cyrano de Bergerac, Captain Brassbound — all beckoned but none was answered.

The stability and social acceptance which the theatre enjoyed during Irving's lifetime tend to obscure an even more important characteristic of his era. These years mark the summit of theatregoing as a popular pastime: more theatres were built, more people attended them, more actors earned a living in them, than in any previous or subsequent period, and if the sum total of plays presented fell somewhat short of the preceding fifty years, this again was evidence of prosperity, since the long run cut out the nightly or weekly change of bill. Responsibility for this state of affairs was by no means solely Irving's or any individual's. Social, economic, and cultural forces conspired to make the years 1865—1914 uniquely receptive to the theatre in Britain. The prejudice which kept so many respectable patrons away from any place of entertainment steadily declined in the second half of the century. Without that change in attitude, not only would Irving and his fellow actor-managers have played to empty stalls (if indeed the stall could have survived at all); there would have been no touring-circuit for them to follow and no new theatres for them to grace.

But this return of the 'quality' to the theatre was not marked, as it had been at the Restoration, by the rapid departure of humbler men, leaving the playhouse to a côterie of courtiers. Irving's audience drew its strength from every class and every calling, and his repertoire, with its emphasis on the spectacular and the sensational, recognised the claims of the gallery as firmly as those of the stalls. It was on this point above all that he parted company with Shaw and those who urged him to tackle something new and contemporary. Ibsen at the Lyceum might or might not have suited Irving and Ellen Terry; it would unquestionably have alienated the Lyceum public, and what was true of the Lyceum was no less true of the St James's or Her Majesty's.

Undoubtedly the actor-managers of Irving's era were fortunate in their generation; they found a public ready to be entertained and looking to the theatre for that entertainment. They had many battles to fight, and far more surrendered than survived, but competition from cheaper and more accessible forms of entertainment was not one of their problems. Indeed the emergence of the music-hall, the most important new development in the entertainment world during these years, was a positive help to the theatres, partly by drawing off the rowdier public which had often impeded artistic progress earlier in the century, and partly by providing cross-fertilisation in such fields as pantomime and musical comedy.

On the other hand the moving picture left Irving's public virtually untouched, since it appeared too late to affect him. By the year of his death, however, the writing on the wall could be read. The showing of films was no longer confined to a music-hall turn; and the era of the purpose-built cinema and purpose-made feature film was not far off. For this reason, if for no other, Irving's period and Irving's achievement were unique; never again would the stage-actor command the public and the publicity that he did. The claims on both audience and journalism of films and film-stars would shortly take over.

The consequence for the drama was slowly but surely to convert it into a minority art. As the cinema began to assume the role in mass-entertainment that the theatre and music-hall had previously undertaken, so the theatrical profession was compelled to reassess its function. The fact that the cinema was 'silent' for the first thirty years of its existence greatly assisted that reassessment. The stage could never hope to compete with the screen in offering spectacle, action, movement, romance. It could offer speech and the theatrical elements to which speech is essential: thought, argument, wit, poetry.

Thus, because of a technical advance, the foundations of Irving's empire crumbled and fell. Melodrama and spectacle were theatrical forms of which speech formed only a minimal part; they commanded their audiences' eyes rather than their ears. But melodrama and spectacle were the basis of Irving's art, both as actor and manager, and of the art of those who followed his lead. Conversely speech was the key to the new intellectual drama — whether psychological, as in Ibsen's analysis of the mysterious springs of human conduct; discursive, as in Shaw's inspired tub-thumping; or poetic, as in Shakespeare when directed by a Poel or a Granville-Barker. In each case the approach differed totally from that of Irving and the Romantic style he practised.

Irving's death at the moment when Shaw's star and that of the New Drama were so firmly in the ascendant marked not merely the passing of a unique performer and leader but the passing of a theatrical era. The finality of his death was at once apparent. No one could replace him, and those who sought to name his successor were doing both Irving and the successor a grave injustice, whether their choice was Tree, Forbes-Robertson, or Irving's own son, Harry. The end of the era was less apparent, since the world he fostered and the public that fostered him did not disappear overnight, and there were plenty of actor-managers, besides the three mentioned, to carry on his work. But as competition increased — from new men with new methods, above all from the new medium of the cinema — the taste which Irving had satisfied lost its savour. The Lyceum itself was never again to know a master like him. For two years after his departure it stood empty and ownerless; then it was rebuilt and opened as a music-hall.

Of the many men who graced the Victorian stage, Henry Irving's name and reputation have unquestionably come to embody those qualities generally associated with Victorian drama and the Victorian theatre, although he did not achieve success until half Victoria's reign was over, and consequently never played for her in a theatre. Nevertheless the association is entirely apt, for apart from his unrivalled record at the Lyceum and his unique standing as the first actor-knight, he has an even stronger though less tangible claim to public recognition as *the* Victorian actor: his appearance. There can seldom if ever have been a performer whose image so successfully suggested the theatre theatrical. His portraits, whether in costume or as Henry Irving (a part he played as potently as any character), stir the imagination. Even his photographs, greatly as he disliked them, hold the onlooker as firmly and with much the same strange power and glittering eye as the Ancient Mariner held the Wedding Guest. To see Irving's likeness is to feel his spell, however indirectly. Though we can never watch him on film, and the few crude and fragmentary recordings of his voice that survive leave us half-deaf and wholly defeated, the face, the features, and the form still beckon us to enter his kingdom — the kingdom of mystery, of magic, of a world we can glimpse but only dream of sharing — the world of Henry Irving.

NOTES

1  Laurence Irving, *Henry Irving*, p. 410.
2  Christopher St John (Editor), *Ellen Terry and Bernard Shaw: A Correspondence* (1949), pp. 383-87. Shaw's original comment was: 'The truth is Irving was interested in nothing but himself, and the self in which he was interested was an imaginary self in an imaginary world. He lived in a dream.'
3  Ibid.

# Select Bibliography

The place of publication is London unless otherwise stated.

*General Surveys include:*

Nicoll, Allardyce, *A History of English Drama 1660 – 1900,* Vol. V: Late Nineteenth-Century Drama 1850 – 1900, revised edition (Cambridge, 1959).
  *English Drama* 1900 – 1930: The Beginnings of the Modern Period (Cambridge, 1973).
  Indispensable hand-lists of plays.
Leech, Clifford, and Craik, T.W. (General Editors), with contributions by Michael R. Booth and others, *The Revels History of Drama in English,* Vol. VI: 1750 – 1880 (1975).
Craik, T.W. (General Editor), with contributions by Hugh Hunt and others, Vol. VII: 1880 to the Present Day (1978).
Rowell, George, *The Victorian Theatre 1792 – 1914,* revised edition (Cambridge, 1978).
  Comprehensive bibliography.

*Illustrated Surveys of some aspects of the subject include:*

Booth, Michael R., *English Melodrama* (1965).
  *Victorian Spectacular Theatre* (1981).
Forbes, Bryan, *That Despicable Race: A History of the British Acting Tradition* (1980).

175

# SELECT BIBLIOGRAPHY

Mander, Raymond, and Mitchenson, Joe, *The Theatres of London* (1961).
   *A Picture History of Gilbert and Sullivan* (1962).
   *The Lost Theatres of London* (1968).
   *Musical Comedy: A Story in Pictures* (1969).
   *Pantomime: A Story in Pictures* (1973).
   *British Music-Hall*, revised edition (1974).
Speaight, Robert, *Shakespeare on the Stage* (1973).


*Of the many Studies of Henry Irving the following are cited:*

Craig, E. Gordon, *Henry Irving* (1930).
Hughes, Alan, 'Henry Irving's Finances: The Lyceum Accounts 1878−1899' in
   *Nineteenth-Century Theatre Research* I: 2 (Edmonton, Alberta, 1973).
   'The Lyceum Staff: A Victorian Theatrical Organization' in *Theatre Notebook*
   XXVIII:1 (1974).
   'Henry Irving's Artistic Use of Stage Lighting' in *Theatre Notebook* XXXIII: 3
   (1979).
   *Henry Irving, Shakespearean* (Cambridge, 1981).
Irving, Laurence, *Henry Irving: The Actor and his World* (1951).
Jones, Henry Arthur, *The Shadow of Henry Irving* (1931).
Saintsbury, H.A., and Palmer, Cecil, (Editors), *We Saw Him Act* (1939).
Stoker, Bram, *Personal Reminiscences of Henry Irving* (1906).
The Percy Fitzgerald Collection of material relating to Irving (22 volumes) in the
Library of the Garrick Club has been drawn on extensively for illustrations.


*Other Studies of and by leading actors in the period include:*

Alexander, George, *Sir George Alexander and the St James's Theatre* by A.E.W. Mason
   (1935).
   'Wyndham and Alexander' by George Rowell in *The Rise and Fall of the Matinée
   Idol* ed. Anthony Curtis (1974).
Bancroft, Squire and Marie, *Mr and Mrs Bancroft On and Off the Stage* (1889).
Benson, Frank, *Benson and the Bensonians* by J.C. Trewin (1960).
Craig, E. Gordon, *Index to the Story of My Days* (1957).
Du Maurier, Gerald, *Gerald* by Daphne Du Maurier (1934).
Harvey, John Martin, *Autobiography* (1933).
   *The Last Romantic* by M. Willson Disher (1948).
Kean, Charles and Ellen, *Emigrant in Motley: Unpublished Letters* ed. J.M.D. Hardwick
   (1954).
Kendal, Madge, *Dame Madge Kendal: By Herself* (1933).
Robertson, Johnston Forbes, *A Player Under Three Reigns* (1925).
Terry, Ellen, *Four Lectures on Shakespeare* (1932).
   *Memoirs*, ed. Edith Craig and Christopher St. John (1933).
   *Ellen Terry and Bernard Shaw: A Correspondence,* ed. Christopher St John (new
   edition, 1949).
   *Ellen Terry* by Roger Manvell (1968).

Tree, Herbert Beerbohm, *Beerbohm Tree: His Life and Laughter* by Hesketh Pearson (1956).
    *The Great Lover: The Life and Art of Beerbohm Tree* by Madeleine Bingham (1979).
Wyndham, Charles, *Charles Wyndham and Mary Moore* by Mary Moore (1925).
    'Wyndham of Wyndham's' by George Rowell in *The Theatrical Manager in England and America* ed. Joseph W. Donohue Jr. (Princeton, 1971).
    *All On Stage: Charles Wyndham and the Alberys* by Wendy Trewin (1980).

*Studies of and by writers in the period include:*

Gilbert, W.S., *Gilbert, Sullivan and D'Oyly Carte* by François Cellier and C. Bridgeman (1914).
    *W.S. Gilbert: His Life and Letters* by Sidney Dark and Rowland Grey (1923).
    *W.S. Gilbert: His Life and Strife* by Hesketh Pearson (1957).
    *Gilbert Before Sullivan* ed. Jane W. Stedman (1967).
    *Gilbert and Sullivan Papers* ed. James Helyar (Lawrence, Kansas, 1971).
    *W.S. Gilbert* by Max Keith Sutton (Boston, 1975).
Sullivan, Arthur, *Sir Arthur Sullivan: His Life, Letters and Diaries* by Herbert Sullivan and Newman Flower, revised edition (1950).
Jones, Henry Arthur, *The Renascence of the English Drama* (1895).
    *The Life and Letters of Henry Arthur Jones* by Doris Arthur Jones (1930).
    *Henry Arthur Jones and the Modern Drama* by R.A. Cordell (New York, 1932).
Pinero, Arthur Wing, *The Social Plays of Arthur Wing Pinero* ed. Clayton Hamilton, 5 vols (New York, 1917).
    *Arthur Wing Pinero* by Walter Lazenby (New York, 1972).
    *The Collected Letters of Sir Arthur Pinero* ed. J.P. Wearing (Minneapolis, 1974).
Planché, James Robinson, *Extravaganzas*, 5 vols (1879).
Shaw, G.B., *Our Theatres in the Nineties*, 3 vols (1932).
    *Major Critical Essays* (1932).
    *Prefaces* (1938).
    *Shaw and Ibsen* ed. J.L. Wisenthal (Toronto, 1979).
Wilde, Oscar, *Aspects of Wilde* by Vincent O'Sullivan (1936).
    *The Life of Oscar Wilde* by Hesketh Pearson (1946).
    *The Letters of Oscar Wilde* ed. Rupert Hart-Davis (1962).
    *The Plays of Oscar Wilde* by Alan Bird (1977).
    *Oscar Wilde* by H. Montgomery Hyde (1977).
    *Oscar Wilde: Art and Egotism* by Rodney Shewan (1977).

*Studies of and by critics and other leading theatrical figures in the period include:*

Archer, William, *English Dramatists of Today* (1882).
    *Real Conversations* (1904).
    *Play-Making* (1912).
    *The Old Drama and the New* (1923).
Beerbohm, Max, *Around Theatres* (1953).

# SELECT BIBLIOGRAPHY

Grein, J.T., *J.T. Grein: The Story of a Pioneer* by Michael Orme (1936).
   *J.T. Grein: Ambassador of the Theatre* N.H.G. Schoonderwoerd (Assen, 1963).
James, Henry, *The Scenic Art* ed. Allan Wade (1949).
Poel, William, *William Poel and the Elizabethan Revival* by Robert Speaight (1954).


*Other sources cited:*

Courtney, W.L., *The Passing Hour* (1925).
Fay, Frank, *Towards a National Theatre: Dramatic Criticism* ed. Robert Hogan, Irish
    Theatre Series 1 (Dublin, 1970).
Hicks, Seymour, *Between Ourselves* (1930).
Hunt, Hugh, *The Abbey: Ireland's National Theatre 1904 – 1979* (Dublin, 1979).
Lorenzen, Richard, 'The Old Prince of Wales's Theatre' in *Theatre Notebook* XXV: 4
    (1971).
Millward, Jessie, *Myself and Others* (1923).
*Report of the Select Committee on Theatrical Licences and Regulations* (1866).
Rowell, George, *Victorian Dramatic Criticism* (1971).
   'Tree's Shakespeare Festivals 1905 – 1913' in *Theatre Notebook* XXIX: 2 (1975).
   *Queen Victoria Goes to the Theatre* (1978).
Southern, Richard, 'The Picture-Frame Proscenium of 1880' in *Theatre Notebook V:* 3
    (1951).
Stottlar, J.F., 'Hardy vs. Pinero: Two Stage Versions of *Far from the Madding Crowd'*
    in *Theatre Survey* 18:2 (New York, 1977).
Trewin, J.C., *The Edwardian Theatre* (Oxford, 1976).
Watson, A.E.T., *A Sporting and Dramatic Career* (1918).
Watson, Mary Jane, *The Independent Theatre Movement in London 1891 – 1914* M.Litt.
    thesis, University of Bristol, 1970).

# Index